The Cycle of Life

The Cycle of Life

An Autobiographical Journey
from Apartheid South Africa to
Britain of a College Principal

Ahmed Choonara OBE

2017000810

Matador
9 Priory Business Park,
Wistow Road, Kibworth Beauchamp,
Leicestershire. LE8 0RX
Tel: 0116 279 2299
Email: books@troubador.co.uk
Web: www.troubador.co.uk/matador
Twitter: @matadorbooks

ISBN 978 1788038 669

British Library Cataloguing in Publication Data.
A catalogue record for this book is available from the British Library.

Printed and bound in the UK by 4edge limited
Typeset in 12pt Minion Pro by Troubador Publishing Ltd, Leicester, UK

Matador is an imprint of Troubador Publishing Ltd

This book is dedicated to family, friends and those who struggled to give birth to a democratically elected South African Government.

ACKNOWLEDGEMENTS

I have been exceedingly fortunate over six decades to have had the unqualified support of my immediate family, beginning in Apartheid South Africa and continuing in a freer England.

I embarked on this project when Liz stated that she wished her late father wrote his full autobiography and suggested that I start mine. I was further encouraged by my nephew's daughter, Doctor Halima Choonara, who wrote a short biography about my brother 'Doc'. Her brother, Mohammed, helped correct some early errors. My brother Ismail provided continuous support and encouragement on this journey. Jane my first wife and Elizabeth (Liz) my second wife, have given me enormous support over the years and in writing this, despite my idiosyncrasies and short comings. Without this, I am certain, I would not have written this biography. Any errors, omissions, interpretation and opinions expressed are my sole responsibility.

CONTENTS

PREFACE

I was born in South Africa and at the age of twenty came to Great Britain to further my education. Since then, with a short spell working overseas, I have made this my home. On this long journey across continents, I have had the good fortune of meeting teachers, students, lecturers, colleagues, neighbours and strangers whose kindness has been spontaneous and generous, helping me in many different ways. They have contributed to my understanding of the principles underpinning the concepts of justice, fair play, respect and compassion. By their actions, they made me aware that there is only one discrimination that can be justified and that is discrimination against discrimination itself. Their guidance and influence has also provided me with the necessary resolve and strength to confront injustice and unfairness directly despite the short term difficulties that this may bring about. They also contributed to my progress in work, starting as an Assistant Lecturer and gradually rising to become the first College Principal in the UK from an Asian heritage background.

Once I embarked on this project of writing about my life experiences, I realised how circumstances (some of your own making and others where you have little or no control over) present you with choices (some easy to make and others forced upon you) and these very choices have consequences (some of which can be enjoyable/tolerable, whilst others can create great difficulties for you and you have to either endure or cope with them by making the necessary adjustment both in terms of day to day activities and expectations). Whilst this is abundantly obvious, we fail to pose this essential question of choice and the likely consequences arising from this before we embark on different episodes of our life. In brief, the collision of your own choices and circumstances with those you have very little control over can lead to consequences determining your future life with the possibility of perverse or positive outcomes.

Visiting one's past is always a matter of remembering accurately the events that shaped that past as well as interpreting it with a degree of humility and honesty. In doing this, I have tried to avoid exaggerations and embellishments, in so far as possible, as well as steer clear of events which might embarrass others, if my recollection was not correct. I sincerely hope that sharing my story with others enables them to avoid the mistakes I have made as well as provide them with the incentives and courage to do things they are capable of achieving.

On this journey, I have also worked with, met and come across some extraordinary people with disadvantages and disabilities far greater than mine and despite that they have distinguished themselves in all walks of life - from sports, academia, science, and employment. They have been inspirational in allowing me to understand a very simple, yet profoundly important concept: if we focus on abilities and potential instead of disabilities, we encourage individuals to achieve what they are capable of achieving, not only for their own personal benefits but their respective contributions can benefit us all.

CHAPTER ONE

THE EARLY YEARS UNDER APARTHEID

I was not aware of where I was or for how long I had been there but when I opened my eyes, standing almost motionless with red moist eyes and extremely anxious faces staring at me from the bedside, were my two elder brothers and sister with their wives and husband. They informed me, many days later, that their anxiety was related to their concern that I may not recognise them when I opened my eyes. That scene deeply embedded in my memory, brought tears to my eyes as I feared that I was responsible for their obvious great anxiety and worries. They were, however, relieved that I recognised them since the hospital staff had emphasised to them that if and when I opened my eyes, it would be advisable for me to see someone I would recognise in case I suffered from amnesia brought about by the severe head trauma I had experienced. I must have fallen asleep soon after as I cannot recall much after seeing my distressed and then relieved family.

During the next few days, between long spells of sleeping, I attempted to talk and whilst my speech was very slurred, I succeeded in making some simple enquiries to both the staff at the hospital and my father, mother and other members of the family visiting me. I was informed that I was in the ward of the small 'Non-European' part of Hamburg Hospital, which was about three miles from my home town of Roodepoort in South Africa, about 12 miles west of Johannesburg. My speech was obviously affected by my injury and I listened to their different narratives without attempting to say much. They explained to me that there had been a fight between a 'White' family owning an illegal shabeen (selling alcohol to Africans illegally) and some 'Black' customers and that as an innocent 'passer-by' I got caught up in this fracas and was assaulted with a brick to the left side of my head at close proximity. I had lost consciousness immediately and fortunately a friend of the family, living close-by to where the assault took place, rushed me in his car to the hospital. The family were informed and my father and brothers arrived very shortly after that at the hospital. The medical examination was carried out by a surgeon who informed my family that I was in imminent danger since I had a major blood clot in the vicinity of my brain and that I would need an emergency operation to remove it. That very evening they operated on me and whilst they successfully removed the blood clot, the medical staff informed my family that there was a very strong likelihood of some permanent long term damage. They were also informed that had the brick struck a few millimetres further to the right, it could have been fatal. This gradually began to make sense of the 'when', 'why', 'where' and the 'what'. During this most traumatic period of my life, the most enduring memory is that of a wonderful supportive family I had been blessed with.

I soon learnt that as the brick struck my left temple, my right side was paralysed. I was told that, once I was in a reasonably stable condition, I would receive help with my speech (speech therapy) as well as physiotherapy to help me strengthen and use my right leg and my right arm. Slowly my body started to recover. After about three weeks, I attempted to walk and took my first shaky steps with assistance. Speech therapy and physiotherapy also commenced at about this time. Whilst I felt comfortable moving my right arm, I found it difficult to move the fingers of my right hand independently This meant that whilst I was able to grip things, fine movement of the fingers for carrying out simple tasks such as writing, buttoning up my pyjama jacket, picking up small items with my right hand, and other fine movements was no longer possible. At this time, sports and particularly cricket and table tennis were my main leisure interests and I was beginning to be recognised for this. I was devastated to learn that as a result of my injury, it would be very unlikely that I would ever play cricket again. This was the end of my great expectation of playing representative cricket. Throughout this life changing experience, this was the only time I remember sobbing since I loved being involved in sports and particularly cricket.

My speech was beginning to make progress and whilst I was able to stand up with assistance, my right arm and particularly my right hand were still very problematic. After four weeks in hospital, I began to be concerned at being woken up every four hours for an injection. When I enquired the reason for this, the medical staff on duty informed me that it was to

3

relieve the pain which I would experience without it. I informed the doctor responsible for the ward, that I was experiencing no pain at all and that the pain killing injection was not necessary. He agreed to temporarily stop this and review it after a few days. After four weeks, this was my first full night of sleep. I began to make gradual medical progress and after six weeks, the medical staff felt that I was no longer in danger and therefore they discharged me from hospital. I left the hospital with a huge bandage covering the large scar on the top of my head. Disappointingly there was no further speech therapy or physiotherapy available for me at the hospital or locally. Occupational therapy was not available at the hospital. The lack of local facilities for either occupational therapy or physiotherapy was just another example of how Africans and other races classified as 'Non-European' in Apartheid South Africa were treated. As a South African with an Indian heritage, regardless of my personal needs or circumstances, the exit from the hospital meant that I was now personally responsible for any follow-up treatment.

My six weeks stay at Hamburg Hospital was not in an intensive care unit but in a small general ward. During most days there was a member of my family present, particularly my sister Bibi, and whilst my speech was improving, much of the time was spent either sleeping or listening to a family member and friends relating to me some of my past escapades and experiences. I think they did this because they took the issue about brain damage and loss of memory very seriously. Despite my family's fear regarding my memory loss, I was pleased that I remembered most events and episodes of my childhood fairly well. Prior to the brain injury I sustained, I had also broken my hand twice in sporting activities and dislocated my shoulder once.

Over the next few months, I began to walk regularly to strengthen my right leg. My right hand was still very restricted in movement and progress was disappointing. I was very fortunate to have a very supportive family and that prevented me from asking questions such as 'why me' and I simply accepted the situation and tried to make the most of the opportunities that were presented. Even at that stage of my life, I was very independent and rarely asked anyone for help and support during the difficulties I experienced using my right hand. I rapidly learned to cope by making small adjustments when dealing with everyday things. This desire to be regarded and accepted as 'normal' was present very shortly after being discharged from hospital and remained a major feature of my future life. On reflection, perhaps this is a characteristic shared by many people with disabilities.

On the day of this life changing experience, the 14TH December 1958, I was supposed to have been involved in a cricket match, playing as the team's opener and one down bowler. On the Sunday of the match, to the understandable displeasure of the rest of the team, I decided not to play. Instead I decided to spend the day with my cousin Ahmed Said and our friends for his birthday celebration. The decision was partly a result of my great disappointment that having done well in the minor counties trial two weeks prior, both as a batsman and as bowler, I was informed that despite playing better than most of the team eventually selected, at 17 years of age I may be 'too young' for a demanding counties match. Thus instead of playing cricket on that Sunday, the day was spent having a birthday lunch and then 'hanging about'. At approximately 5 p.m., we all decided to go to one of the friends' house to listen to music. This brush with death, with the catastrophic effect on my speech, balance and above all the paralysis of my right hand, had far reaching consequences. This was the beginning of a very long journey.

Whilst much of what I have written above is an accurate account of events that fundamentally changed my life, the narrative of my early childhood is put together either from what I was told by others and/or my own recollections. Once I commenced on this project, I was surprised by how remembering one event triggered off memories of other events which were previously obscured by the myriad of things that occurred later in life.

1941 to 1951

I was born in Roodepoort, South Africa in November, 1941 and my family were South African Asians. My family was relatively large with six brothers and one sister: we were all born in South Africa apart from my late brother 'Doc' who was born in Surat, India in 1922. Members of the family, who were not away studying abroad, lived in our flat above the shop in Station Street, Roodepoort. An interesting aspect of my family is that all my brothers and sister were never together in one place until a family reunion in

2004 in Manchester. There are several elements of my early years I recall clearly. As a child, the segregation and brutality of Apartheid was an 'accepted' part of growing up in South Africa. This fact, however, did not prevent me from enjoying my childhood, my extended family life and building friendships which have lasted a lifetime.

The two events which I can still recall clearly from my childhood surprised me since one was from my very early years and the second one was later but much more dramatic and life threatening. When I was about four years old, I remember a particular Saturday afternoon when all businesses were closed: I was trying to keep up with my brother Ebrahim and his friend by running after them. Ebrahim said "you cannot come with me today to play because later you will be seeing the 'Golden Bird' ". Ignorant of what he meant but still excited, I accepted this and went back to our flat. I soon discovered that the 'Golden Bird' my brother referred to was what the barber, come circumciser, said I needed to look upwards, to see a 'Golden Bird' when he performed his circumcision without anaesthetic. This was my first painful introduction to a world where everything is not what you are told to expect especially 'the Golden Bird'.

Several years passed before the event which almost ended my life in early childhood – my childhood friend Mohammed Valliallah, now a retired doctor, and I picked and ate attractive red berries thinking that they were edible. I must have had a greater quantity than Mohammed because of a dramatic turn of events an hour later – whilst we were playing street-cricket. I bent to pick up the ball and simply collapsed on the ground. I later learnt that I was in a coma for some time and my parents informed me that the berries I ate were poisonous and that I was very fortunate to be alive. The effect on Mohammed was not as severe as he had consumed a lot less than me. This event taught me my second important lesson – even really attractive things are not always what they appear to be.

In addition to our main accommodation, the flat above the shop in Station Street, my father also rented the property next door which was an old fashioned South African bungalow. I recall that my eldest brother Mohammed (later referred to as 'Doc') lived there with my sister-in-law Halima. The back garden also housed a large shed where my brother began to keep a variety of pigeons including racing pigeons. The additional accommodation was also very handy when my late cousins Amina and her brother Ahmed arrived from Mozambique to begin and continue their education. My cousin Ahmed and I began the first years of our schooling at the same time since he was only a day older than me. I recall my brother telling me the story of my uncle from Mozambique phoning my father to inform him that his wife had given birth the day before, to a boy and they called him 'Ahmed' and my father's reply was short and to the point 'same here' and on reflection perhaps he should have simply stated 'ditto'.

As a very young child growing up in 'apartheid' South Africa, you are made aware very early on that there were certain facilities that you were barred from and these were reserved only for the 'white' or 'European' population. Local libraries, swimming pools, parts of the post office, parts of the hospital and almost all public facilities were segregated according to a simple division – 'European' and 'Non-European'. Trains and train stations were segregated with the best facilities inevitably reserved for 'Europeans' despite the fact that most people classified as 'European' were not born in Europe but settlers, their facilities were much superior to those available for the rest of the population. In many instances, facilities such as public libraries, public swimming pools and so on were exclusively for the use of the 'European' population.

My parents and elder siblings regularly reminded me that there were certain areas of the town you did not enter since these were 'European' areas. I recall one incident when I was about ten years of age, my childhood friend Mohammed and I cycled into a 'White' residential area, not far from our home, and we were trapped by about ten white teenagers who cornered us. We were made to stand against the wall and they began pelting us with small pebbles and clay for over half an hour. Our tears and anguish only created great amusement for them. Eventually we were allowed to leave with the threat that if we ever wandered into their residential area again, the treatment we would be subjected to would be far more severe. Despite this unpleasant experience, cycling provided us with the opportunities to explore places outside our immediate environment. On one of these excursions, Mohammed and I agreed to cycle on the road from Roodepoort to Krugersdorp to see how far we could go. We arrived in Krugersdorp, which was eight miles away, tired and hungry. We sought out the

'Asian' area of the town and enquired of the address of a relation Mohammed remembered that he had there. On arriving at this "aunt's" home, we were welcomed and given a drink and a light meal. The "aunt" had the presence of mind to phone our families in Roodepoort and inform them of our whereabouts and reassured them that we would be cycling back after some rest. Most of our other cycle trips were shorter. One of the most popular in summer was along the Randfontein Road with its three bridges. The three bridges were over small streams and in hot weather skinny dipping was an enjoyable outdoor activity for us.

Whilst I was aware of the great disparity in the facilities offered to the different races in South Africa, the most disturbing scene that has been embedded in my mind as a child was witnessing on a regular basis, on the road by our shop, Africans in chains and handcuffs being marched from the police station to the railway station on the way to prison. My father's response to my childhood enquiry about this, situation was that most of the Africans were arrested for 'pass offences' and sentenced, after the briefest appearance in court, to prison. He explain to me that the 'Pass Laws' meant that all male black adult Africans (later extended to women) had to carry a document called the 'Pass Book' which identified the person, his/her address and the permission and reason for that person to be at that particular location. This document had to be carried by black Africans 24/7 and failure to produce it on demand by the police was a criminal offence. The 'Pass Laws' did not apply to any other racial group in South Africa.

As a young person, I regularly witnessed the brutality with which 'European 'policemen enforced this unjust law frequently with batons and police dogs. Growing up in South Africa, many of us assumed that the Pass Laws were introduced and imposed by the Afrikaner (Boers) Nationalist Government under Doctor Malan in 1948 when, in fact, they were introduced in 1913 by the English speaking Government, with support from the UK, to control the influx of black labour to the growing urban areas. The reason for the population drift was very simple since the designated areas for black Africans were very small and not very productive agriculturally and the urban areas provided them with employment opportunities – in their own country. Racial subjugation, racial discrimination, and racial exploitation were part and parcel, after all, of empire building. This pattern of exploitation, with small variations, was similar across Angola and the Americas to Zanzibar and Zambia.

As a child, the segregation and brutality of Apartheid was an 'accepted' part of growing up in South Africa.

When I began writing about my personal experiences and background, I soon realised how little I knew of my father's early life and the epic journey he made in 1906 as an orphan age six, to South Africa. I have been told that as a child he began working in a shop owned by relatives packing paper bags with sugar, salt and flour, weighing them and sealing them for sale in the shops. He gradually built up a reputation as a conscientious worker, which lasted a lifetime, and slowly began saving money to enable him to venture into the business world on his own accord. My father was a gentle, quiet and pragmatic person rarely, if ever, losing his temper. I recall one particular episode as an example of this: at the age of eleven, he 'caught' me smoking a cigarette in the backyard of the shop. I expected, at best, to be severely reprimanded but instead he invited me back into his office and stated 'that if I wanted to be a grown man then I should smoke 'this' and handed me a Havana cigar and lit it. I was repulsed by my first inhalation and coughed violently. I have never smoked since. He never experienced formal education himself and was self-taught both in numeracy and literacy. He worked long hours diligently and began to build up a reputation as a successful entrepreneur and property owner locally. It may be because of his lack of formal education that he valued education for all his children and took a keen interest in their progress and achievements as well as being willing to finance their education, even if it meant that they had to study abroad.

My Late Father and Mother

The major principle he assumed his children would adhere to, was that they concentrated on their education and that they did not marry outside of their faith. Unfortunately, to my understanding of this, he never clearly articulated these concerns. In contrast, my mother was much more liberal and tolerant of her children particularly her last born – me. She tolerated my bad behaviour and never informed my father of this. She indulged my childhood peculiar eating habits such as 'no onions' in my food which resulted in an extra dish to be prepared especially for me. In 1946, my brother Mahmood and about ten youngsters aged ten to twelve years made the journey by boat from South Africa to India to study. Little did we realise that the next time we would meet, it would be in Birmingham, England twenty two years later. After attending college, he was selected to join the Pakistan Air-force and the rest of the family in South Africa followed his rapid career progression with interest and pride.

I started my schooling in Grade One of the Roodepoort Indian School in January 1947. I continued at this school for the next ten years until I passed my Standard Eight (pre Matriculation) Examination. My teachers, in my early years were predominantly from a mixed heritage background, in apartheid South Africa referred to as 'Coloured'. In later years, more 'Asian' teachers joined the staff of the school. Progression in school was organised on the basis that you had to pass each 'end of year' examination to advance to your next class. I was reasonably good academically and progressed each year, mostly in the top four. This, no doubt, pleased my parents and particularly my father immensely. I was happy at school and fairly popular with my peers and most of the teachers since I clearly recall being asked, throughout my school days, to take leading roles in School Concerts, plays and other events. One particular event springs to mind: when I was 14 years of age, Mr. Webb our class teacher asked me to work with him on a project which culminated in a solo performance in the school hall for the whole school, including all the teachers. On the day, I was blind folded and seated on a chair on top of a table in the middle of the hall, and in total silence from over 300 persons I was asked a variety of personal questions about members of staff and events by Mr Webb. Since I was blind folded I could not see who or what he was pointing at and barring one incorrect answer, which added to the authenticity of the mystical powers of Mr Webb and me, I slowly came up with all the correct responses to the great variety of questions he posed, to the amazement of the whole school. Over the next few days, teachers and fellow pupils kept asking me 'how did you do that'? I was sworn to silence and gave nothing away. The clue lay in the way the questions were posed and a very good memory.

Despite growing up in this supportive home and school environment, I was already beginning to understand the great disparity that existed between how the different ethnic groups were being resourced for their education. The 'Whites' (Europeans) were allocated the biggest proportion of the education budget, nationally and locally, despite the fact that they were in a minority compared to the rest of the population. The black Africans were given meagre resources for education despite being the majority population. After World War 2 the Afrikaners (Boers) and their Nationalist Party took over governing the country. Their ideology that all 'black' races were inferior to the 'white' race and the black race must be only educated sufficiently to serve the white race as 'hewers of wood and carriers of water' began to be integrated ruthlessly in the apartheid legislation.

In addition to attending school, almost all Muslim children under the age of sixteen attended the afternoon Madresa (religious school for Muslim children) in the same school buildings. This was the most tiresome, uninteresting and mind numbing experience of my childhood. The major reason for this was that most of the instructions were delivered by people who knew very little about education and consequently used rote learning, without understanding, for their instruction. This problem was further compounded by the lack of literacy in Arabic of both the instructors and the pupils. This then presented some of my contemporaries and me with a problem which we temporarily solved by providing our mothers with plausible reasons why we were unable to attend Madresa on particular days. The chief acceptable excuse was that one or other of my friends had a birthday and the birthday party was that particular afternoon and our attendance was required. It was several years before my mother realised that some of my friends were having multiple birthday parties during the year. Abraham Lincoln's words seem appropriate 'You can fool some of the people all of the time, and all of the people some of the time, but you can not fool all of the people all of the time'. My mother, obviously belonged to the latter category and thus, unfortunately, this birthday lark came to an end and the monotonous rote learning was restored.

In 1948, my parents went for pilgrimage to Saudi Arabia and my brother 'Doc' and my sister-in-law Halima, who were married in 1947, were responsible for our welfare in Roodepoort. My mother returned to South Africa with family friends but my father went to India. As a young person, I was not aware of the significance of this until several years after this event. Unknown to me, at this juncture in my life, my father married a second time. I was only informed of this by my brother Ebrahim three years later. Whilst Muslims are allowed up to four wives with the proviso that they are all treated equally, it was exceptional and unusual in Roodepoort. Obviously, as a child, to be informed that your father has taken a second wife was upsetting but the effect on my mother was much more distressing. It was only in later years that I fully understood why my mother shed so many tears after returning from pilgrimage. The only consolation at the time was that, as far as I was aware, my father treated both of his wives fairly. A short time after my father's marriage, my step-mother arrived in Mozambique and lived in the family property there. My father then began regular visits to Mozambique. My half-brother Gulam was born there. I recall visiting them and was welcomed in their home and Gulam's mother treating me with kindness and generosity. The only time, however, I recall, that my brothers, sister and I were upset was when my father, without any warning, brought my step-mother to Roodepoort. It is also worth noting two elements of this situation: firstly, that after a few years my mother and step-mother began to form a reasonable relationship after my step-mother's visit to Roodepoort and secondly, Gulam was always accepted as a full member of the family and respected as a fellow sibling with all the obligations and rights this warranted.

After returning from his trip to Saudi Arabia and India, my father devoted much of his energy to the construction of the Mare Street flats for the family. The Mare Street flats consisted of five shops on the ground floor, a garage for one car, and six flats above. These flats were the first flats constructed in an area of Roodepoort populated predominantly by Asians. The Station Street area was also populated by Asians but sparsely since this area was dominated by shops. My second eldest brother 'Yussof' (referred to as 'Joe') having returned to Roodepoort from his studies in Aligarh decided that it was time to settle down and get married. He married Fatima (referred to as 'Appa') in 1949. In July 1950, at the age of nine, I became an uncle for the first time with the birth of Azra to my brother Joe and his wife Appa. I became known to my nieces and nephews as 'Nalla Papa' meaning small uncle. In the same year my brother Ismail departed for India to further his education. It was also around this period that my young cousins and I spent some of our summer holidays with my father's friends, the Mosams, in the rural town of Nylstroom. The Mosam family and our family continued their friendship and a few years later my father agreed to go into partnership with them to construct a three story apartment block in Mozambique. This friendship continued when both families had young people studying in the UK and Ireland.

CHAPTER TWO

TRAUMA, TRAGEDY AND TRANSFORMATION

The decade 1951 to 1961 was one of the most momentous for my family and me. My eldest brother Mohammed (later known as 'Doc')was restless working in the family shop. One day he stumbled upon an advert offering free scholarships for studying medicine in Dhaka, East Pakistan. He applied for this scholarship and was accepted to study medicine at Medical College in Dhaka. 'Doc' left South Africa in 1950-51 for Dhaka, in what was then known as 'East Pakistan' (now 'Bangladesh') to resume his lifelong ambition to become a medical doctor. This was his second trip overseas to study. The first trip occurred in the 1940's to Aligarh in India, where he matriculated and attended Aligarh Muslim University. This first period of study was unfortunately interrupted by distractions, particularly spending time at the races in Bombay instead of putting more effort into his studies, and my father learning of this, requested that he returned to South Africa. In 1951, I became an 'Uncle' for the second time when Halima gave birth to a son named 'Nazir in February 1951.

In June 1951, the whole family moved to the 'Choonara Flats', as they became known locally. A major characteristic of the flats was that instead of a small narrow passage leading to each flat, my father saw the possibilities of a wide covered area stretching from the first flat to the fifth flat as an important social and domestic space for all the occupants of the flat. This wide and long veranda soon became known as 'The Stoep' partly to differentiate it from the veranda in the front of the flat. As a family, and particularly as children, we spent many hours on the 'stoep'. If there was a large family function such as a planned wedding, then several close families would gather for days on the flat preparing and this then would give rise to evening meals taken on the 'stoep' since it had the capacity to seat anything from 20 to 100 at one sitting. As a child, this long 'stoep' also provided us with the opportunity to organise a variety of games and sports such as cricket, table tennis, and soccer. When several of my friends joined us, we would organised a 'Sports Day' on the 'stoep' including a variety of races, relays, long jumps, and high jumps.

The first flat was occupied by my parents, my brother Ebrahim, my sister Fatima, known as 'Bibi' and me. This flat was the hub of the family since all meals for the whole family were cooked and consumed there. The small kitchen, with its cast iron coal stove and engraving 'Union NO 7' on the oven door, was the central focus and in winter all the brothers tried to manoeuvre as close as possible to it. In the flat, my father and mother occupied the main bedroom, my brother Ebrahim and I shared the second bedroom and my sister had the third bedroom. For a short period of time Flat 2 was occupied by my sister-in-law Halima and my nephew Nazir. One of the longest occupants of Flat 3 was my brother Joe and his family. The other flats were occupied by a variety of Muslim tenants including the Timol family. The Timol family occupied the second flat for a number of years and I became good friends with Ahmed Timol, who was the same age as me. I intend to discuss this later. One of the immense joys of living on the flat was the close family ties that developed and particularly for me was the wonderful experience of witnessing four of my nieces, Azra, Raziya, Zaheeda and Yasmin growing up. Each of them were strong characters in their own way and, as the youngest uncle, I was privileged to build up a wonderful rapport with each of them.

A year later, my sister in law Halima and my nephew Nazir, joined my brother in Dhaka. It was there that my second nephew 'Imtiaz' was born in 1953. In 1954, my brother Ismail returned to South Africa for a short period. In that same year he departed for England to further his studies and subsequently became a science teacher and later a lecturer at a London teacher training college. Little did I realise then, that his foresight and determination was going to be so instrumental in changing my life in the future. It is also worth noting that he was the first member of the Choonara family to begin life in England. During the period from 1951 to 1956, my brother 'Doc' devoted much of his time to his medical education and graduated as a doctor. His return to South Africa was very brief since the South African apartheid Government did not recognise his qualifications and he could not practice there. As a result in December 1956, he departed for England. 'Doc' and his family played an important part in my future and I will come to this later.

Growing up with an extended family and close friends in Roodepoort in the early 1950s was exciting despite the oppression of apartheid. In the absence of accessible sports facilities other than a sports ground for adults, we created our own amusements and games. The school playground games included a variety of marble and spinning top games, highly competitive at most times. Street games included 'street cricket', 'street football', 'gillie dundie' played with two different lengths of sticks (I think this was a game originating from India), and 'three tins' which comprised of three empty fruit tins stacked one above the other and two teams, one at each end of the street had to knock down the tins with a tennis ball. Once the tins were down, the opposing team had to chase and strike each of the opposing team members with a ball. One major advantage of growing up in a relatively warm climate was that we spent much of our free time outdoors with friends.

Towards the end of December 1954, during the long summer school holidays, my first cousin Ahmed, my second cousin Essop (known as 'Essopie') and I travelled by the overnight train from Johannesburg to Lourenco Marques, in Mozambique (now known as 'Maputo') for a holiday. As thirteen year olds, going independently of adults, to another country was obviously exciting and the first few days, staying with my uncle was indeed enjoyable. Little did I anticipate that this holiday was heading for a tragedy which would have major repercussions not only on my life but also on my second cousin's family. On the 4th January 1954, the three of us agreed to go to a swimming complex for the day. Besides a cafeteria, the complex which was situated in extensive grounds, had a pool for children and a full size adult pool. There were no other visitors to the complex at that time. Since none of us were capable swimmers, we spent much of our time in the pool for children. After spending sometime in this pool, my cousin Ahmed and I sat talking on the grass close to the pool and unbeknown to us my second cousin Essopie wandered over to the adult pool and went in. After a few minutes, we realised that Essopie was no longer in the pool for children and we began looking for him. As we walked over to the adults' pool, we saw a figure going under the water and within a few seconds we realised that it was Essopie and we tried to grab him from the side of the pool and began screaming realizing that he was in trouble. After several long minutes two young Portuguese men arrived and realised what was happening and dived into the pool in an effort to rescue Essopie. Whilst they brought Essopie to the surface and tried to resuscitate him, it was to no avail. The next few days were traumatic not only for Essopie's and our respective families but also for my cousin Ahmed and me. We had to replay that tragic event, over and over again, to all the members of the family and others who rightly wanted to know of the circumstances which led to the drowning of Essopie. For nearly two decades after that event, I refused to go into either a swimming pool or the sea for a swim. The impact on Essopie's younger brother, Ahmed Said was much longer lasting and he began swimming only in recent years. A summer holiday, which began so promisingly and ended in a tragedy, is as a vivid memory now as it was then.

Returning home to Roodepoort after this tragic event was no easy matter, since all our mutual friends wished to know what had occurred and I had to recount this tragic event frequently over the ensuing weeks.

After a period of time, life was beginning to be as normal as could be with school, madresa, sports and family events taking up most of my time. During the period 1954 to December 1955, my brother Ebrahim and my sister Bibi were in serious relationships with their respective spouses to be. In an age long before mobile phones and texting, this provided me with an enterprising opportunity. In a period when family life was still along the traditional lines, open courtship was a 'no-no' and couples met in relative secrecy. This meant that a courier for communications was necessary whose presence did not arouse suspicion from either partner's families. I frequently acted as a courier, charging the sender of the message a small fee, and unbeknown to either party, I was also able to charge a small fee to the recipient before they received the message. Unfortunately this enterprise was short-lived because my brother Ebrahim married Khatija Valliallah (referred to as 'Choti') on 25 December 1955 and my sister Bibi married Solly on 26 December 1955. Their respective marriages meant that from then onwards I enjoyed the benefits of a bedroom of my own.

My early memory of the marriage of my brother Ebrahim was when his new wife 'Choti' was preparing a light Sunday dinner in Flat Number 1 and was warming up some hot oil in a frying pan and I idiotically embarked on an experiment which went hideously wrong. I asked my friend Mohammed Valliallah, who was with me in our small kitchen 'what would happen to an egg if I put the whole egg in the hot oil without removing the shell?' I put the egg in the oil to see what would happen and just then 'Choti' was approaching the stove and the egg exploded and scalded her hand with hot oil and she screamed. The magnitude of my stupidity was immediately apparent to me Mohammed and I made a very, hasty exit from the flats. 'Choti' rapidly received treatment for her burns and unfortunately my friend Mohammed received punishment from the elder brother of 'Choti' for something he was simply a bystander to. I was reprimanded by almost everyone in the family and learnt an important lesson: that it is important to consider the different consequences which could result from embarking on a new experiment, before you commence on the experiment.

The second marriage, that of my sister, provided me an opportunity to participate in a fairly lucrative traditional practice in Roodepoort at that time: when the marriage ceremony was performed in the local mosque, my prospective brother-in-law had to leave his new shoes near the entrance, which then provided me with an opportunity to temporarily remove them and I only returned them when the ransom of £5 was paid. This was a tidy sum of money for a young teenager in those days. The following year, my enterprising activities took a different turn: my two sisters-in-law and my sister were all very keen on reading romantic comics but would not be seen purchasing them and this provided me with an opportunity. I would purchase second hand romantic comics from a small bookshop for 6p and charge each of them 3p to read them and return to me. After they completed their reading and returned the comic to me, I doubled the profit by trading in the comic for 3p. Since their enthusiasm for romantic comics lasted for at least two years, this was a profitable enterprise with very little risk and no taxes to pay for a fourteen years young entrepreneur.

In 1956, I attended and successfully completed Standard 8 (pre-matriculation examination) of the Roodepoort Indian School. The school was refused permission by the Apartheid Government from extending its provision by two additional years which would allow successful students to progress to university. Previously many successful Indian students progressed their academic life by attending the final two years at the Johannesburg Indian High School. Unfortunately for me and my contemporaries, the refusal of allowing Indian students to progress their academic life in proximity to their respective homes or by attending Johannesburg Indian High School was part of the pernicious policy of the Apartheid Government which wanted all Indians to move away from their normal habitat and live in Lenasia, an area designated specifically for Indians under the 'Group Areas Act'. The area designated was then a wilderness called 'Lense' approximately 20 miles from Roodepoort and Johannesburg. This presented a problem both for me and my father. My father wanted me to continue my education and so did I, but unfortunately the options were very limited. There were schools locally where we lived, and in most circumstances and places in the world, I would have been able to continue my education progressing on to university and pursuing a successful career. I was, however, in South Africa and normality rarely existed for Black and Asian people and all the high schools locally were only for 'white' people. I attended a voluntary high school for a brief period but the curriculum was very limited and we realised that this was not going to further my education. My father considered sending me to overseas to further my education but that was put on hold when my brother Ismail married Kasia in England in December 1957. My father was gravely disappointed about this event since Kasia was not a Muslim. This was a major rift in our family as far as my father was concerned but the rest of us in Roodepoort were all very pleased for my brother and Kasia.

I started working in our family shop as a very junior sales assistant. The shop was a general dealer selling soft goods as well as groceries. The shop built a reputation as a specialist in imported wool predominantly from England. This was obviously a seasonal demand focusing on autumn and winter peak trade. Our knitting customers were from all sectors of society. When trade was slow and there was little to do in the shop, my brother Ebrahim, the assistant, Yussof and I played cricket in the aisles with a table tennis ball and the cardboard tubes used for rolling cloth. This indulgence only occurred when my father was out of the shop and any of us sighting him approaching would holler "rain stop play". My brother Ebrahim was a gifted cricketer representing the regional and provincial Asian team on a number of occasions as a left-handed batsman and wicket keeper. My brother Yussof (also known as 'Joe') was normally in charge of the business in my father's absence. His great passion in the shop was the buying and especially selling his personal postage stamp collection. One of the other features of our family life, applicable also in the shop, was the strict hierarchical code on such things as who has access to newspapers first, and so on. An interesting feature of 'shop life' then was that twice a day there were tea breaks. Since tea was never brewed in the shop, the African delivery man working for the family, had to make the journey twice a day on his delivery cycle to our home to fetch two large hot metal teapots. He balanced this on the each side of the handlebar for a mile and never failed or faltered.

The events of 14th December 1958 and the severe head trauma I experienced meant that during much of 1959 I was preoccupied with making adjustments to my new and restricted life.

In 1959, after consulting our GP, I was referred to a private neuro-surgeon in Johannesburg to explore the possibility of restoring the use of my right hand. The facilities of the neuro-surgeon were situated in the 'all white' clinic across the road from the 'Non-European' section of the Johannesburg General Hospital. Prior to the exploratory surgery, I was admitted to 'Non-European' section of the hospital for preparation including taking an angiogram of my head/brain. I was taken to the hospital by my brother Ebrahim and his friend Yussof. I was now more familiar with hospitals than either of them and relaxed, whilst they were obviously nervous for me, and the admission officer asked them to my amusement 'which one of you two is having this operation?' This was the starting of an eventful process. The medical staff involved in administering the angiogram were all of a non-Muslim faith and being in a semi-conscious state I was informed later that during this process I kept pointing to the medical staff and muttering 'Your God, My God, Our God'. This was a real surprise to me since I was the least religious person in the family. One beneficial outcome arising from this was that the 'White' Matron thought I must be endowed with something holy and therefore informed all the nurses that there must not be any restrictions on my visiting hours and that I must be treated as a VIP. The actual exploratory surgery was completed in the 'White' Clinic and I was subsequently pushed across the road to the 'Non-European' section of the hospital. Nothing positive emanated from this exploratory surgery and after about two weeks, I was discharged. Shortly after returning home from this exploratory procedure, I had a most frightening experience – extremely violent convulsions to the right side of my body. My arms, hands and upper torso shook regularly and violently, so that for the first and only time in my life I thought I was about to die. The family GP arrived very rapidly and after consulting colleagues, he prescribed a drug, I think was called 'Epinutern' which gradually reduced and then eliminated the violent convulsions. I was kept on this drug for a few years and suffered no recurrence of convulsions since 1959.

Whilst I once again began to work in the family shop, my contribution was limited by being the youngest person there. This fact did not prevent me from being involved with other available opportunities including taking my driving test and passing it on the first attempt.

However, life in Roodepoort whilst occupied, doing everyday things such as going to work in our family business, going to the cinema, courting a number of girlfriends, watching sporting events, enjoying witnessing my four nieces growing up on the flat and being involved in other minor social activities, my life was beginning to drift pointlessly without any long term aim. The only new personal and surprising event during this period was that after I sent a short typed letter to a potential pen pal in Poland, I received a reply from a girl called Krystina. I never thought that there would ever be an opportunity for us to meet in the future but nevertheless I continued corresponding with her.

Unearthed my Learner's Driving Licence from 1959

In this period one particular sporting event which I recall clearly and which gave many of us great pleasure was the first and only time the full 'White' South African team played a full 'Non-European team at cricket. The 'Non-European' team included Basil D'Oliveria and my neighbour and good friend Ahmed Timol. The result was that the 'White' South African team, which was recognised internationally, was defeated in the match. The Apartheid Government were mortified that the match took place and more importantly, the 'White' team lost. Since this undermined the very basis of Apartheid, the superiority of the 'White' race. The Apartheid Government banned all further inter-racial sporting events.

In March of 1960 the killing of 69 black South Africans as well the injury suffered by another 400, the majority of them shot in the back by white policemen was one of the great atrocities committed by the apartheid government and widely reported. The Sharpeville Massacre was a turning point in my political education especially since the people of this small township, about 35 miles from Johannesburg, were simply protesting against the iniquitous Pass Laws. This was also a major turning point for the ANC. This then was when I began to realise that the Apartheid Government would use all its might and apparatus against protests to preserve the injustice of its privileged position. This event also gave me some direction and I began to take an active interest in the political situation in Apartheid South Africa. The 'Study Circle' in Roodepoort, organised by more senior contemporaries, particularly Ahmed Bhabha, included my friends Ahmed Timol, Cassim Bhabha and Yussof Saloojee, and was my early initiation into active politics since 'politics' was the main focus of its discussion and activities. My early forays in this was distributing political leaflets calling for strike action, lookout duties while others distributed leaflets, making clandestine phone calls from public phone boxes for others to participate in strike action and so on. These minor activities were perceived as major threats to the Apartheid regime and therefore illegal and punishable with imprisonment. After all, the essence and tension of Apartheid was about the privilege and appearance of a white 'civilised' society against the stark reality and brutality of the everyday lives of black, coloured and Asian South Africans.

In October 1961, my father wrote to my three brothers overseas asking them of their intentions regarding the estate and what their respective wishes were. This was an important event as far as the family were concerned since this act indicated my father's wish to integrate my brother Ismail back into the family. I subsequently learnt that Ismail was planning to come to South Africa to discuss this but was waiting for a visa. The run up to Christmas was a busy period in the shop but on Sunday the 16th December a tragic family event occurred, which at the time was totally unexpected, and which had major consequences for the whole family and particularly me. As usual, after spending five and half days hard at work, on this Sunday my father was playing 'bridge' with his friends at the Roodepoort Indian Club. He was very fit and I cannot recall a time when he was ill and had to spend time in bed. His playing partners at the club included a G.P. and sometime around midday he began to complain of a nagging pain on the right side of his chest. His medical friend suggested that he takes some analgesics and rest at home with the assurance that if the pain persisted, he must call him. He returned home and was preparing to go to bed. My brothers

Joe and Ebrahim informed me that our father was not well and I was not to take the car in case there was a need to use it for my father. My room on the flat was adjacent to my parent's room, and as I approached my room, I heard a strange noise emanating from my parent's room. Upon investigating this, I witnessed the most disturbing family scene imaginable – my father on the floor gasping for breath and in the throes of death. I screamed and my brothers rushed to the room and whilst we lifted him onto the bed another member of the family was phoning the G.P. The time interval between when he first complained of the pain on the right side of his chest and me discovering my father on the floor was approximately two hours. My father died of a massive heart attack with very unusual manifestation of symptoms – a pain on the right side of his chest.

As Muslims, we endeavour to bury our dead within twenty four hours and the rest of the day was initially spent frantically phoning friends and relations in South Africa, England, Pakistan, Mozambique and Malawi. The rest of the time was spent preparing for the funeral and prayers. The funeral, a very large event, was held the next day and the whole family was distressed and bewildered by the loss of our father, our guide, role model and compass in this world. Everyday memories of my relationship and activities with my father began to surface. At the age of twenty, my life now was in turmoil with no direction or perceivable future. A week later in December 1961, I was informed that my brother, Ismail was coming over from England to pay his last respects and discuss issues concerning the family. His arrival in late December had momentous consequences on my future life and direction.

After paying his respects to our deceased father and visiting the graveyard where he was buried, my brother Ismail began discussions with other members of the family and me regarding my future. He very quickly determined that I was not very interested or involved in the family business and that the future for me in South Africa was indeed bleak. Since he was working as a school teacher in London and had only a small amount of time in the December of 1961 before he would need to return to work, he used his persuasive powers to convince my family that I would need to go back with him to England. The reasoning behind this was that I may get access to more advanced medical advice in England regarding my right hand than was available to me in South Africa as well as provide me with an opportunity to further my education. Thus events commencing on Sunday 16 December 1961 with our father's death, rapidly and profoundly changed the direction and future for me. My brother, Ismail was instrumental in persuading my family to let me go to England with him and provided me with the opportunity to come to England and to further my education. Thus my gratitude to him is immeasurable. Towards the end of December 1961, the speed of changes in my life left me bewildered and I was both excited and apprehensive of what was to come. Thus in late December my brother and I took the long flight from Jan Smuts Airport in Johannesburg to London to begin a new chapter of my life.

My major regret of leaving South Africa was not being able to complete something I started in about September 1961: I had observed for a number of weeks a young African person, about eighteen years of age, crawling on all fours and begging on Station Street. After some discussions with him I learnt that his name was Albert and that he was born with this deformity. I decided that it would be appropriate to explore whether anything could be medically done for him to enable him to walk. In November 1961 I commenced my search by taking him to our local hospital – Hamburg Hospital – they recommended that I take him to Baraguanna Hospital approximately fifteen miles away, which was the biggest hospital for 'Non-Europeans' in South Africa. Early in December 1961 I took Albert to the Hospital and after examination we were informed that with a number of surgical operations over a lengthy period of time, he may be able to walk with appropriate physiotherapy and training. They suggested that they would make an appointment with a specialist and inform us when to return for discussing this fully and perhaps drawing up a plan of action. The death of our father and my hastily arranged departure to England brought a premature closure to my attempt to assist a fellow human being whose disability and disadvantages were far, far greater than mine. As my departure was imminent, I attempted to persuade friends to take up this but to no avail since all of them were in paid employment and unable to take time off. This failure on my part still haunts me to this day.

My head injury was like an earthquake that suddenly pulled apart the tectonic plates of my drifting life. The sudden and untimely death of my father then precipitated events that brought my brother from England to South Africa and he brought me to England with him, to provide me with opportunities to renew my shattered life.

As I embarked on living in England, the one thought that kept recurring was 'In most situations, one cannot undo what has been done but one can do what needs to be done to improve one's quality of life and help and serve others'.

CHAPTER THREE

A NEW BEGINNING

My flight from Johannesburg to London in late December 1961 was filled with a mixture of trepidation and excitement. Whilst this was my first flight at the age of twenty, my obvious and immediate concern was centred on my ability to cope with living in a relatively 'free society' where access to education, health and all other normal services was not based on the colour of your skin but on your legal entitlement. My first impression of England during the drive at night from the airport to my brother Ismail's one bedroom flat in Fulham was both revealing and disturbing. My preconception of England, formed by reading classical English novels, listening to radio plays and particularly watching historical costume dramas of 'rolling hills and stately homes', was completely shattered by seeing, for the first time, row upon row of terrace houses. It took a considerable amount of time for me to reconcile my preconceived perception of the English landscape with the reality of living in England. Arriving in Fulham I was, however, pleased to meet Kasia, my sister in law and by the expression on her face and her body language, she was both excited and delighted to see Ismail again. My stay in Fulham was a very short one since Ismail and Kasia were both in full time employment. My brother Ismail drove me to Trafford Park, Manchester where I was going to live with my eldest brother 'Doc'.

Arriving at number Four, Fourth Avenue, Trafford Park we were warmly greeted by my brother 'Doc', my sister-in-law, Halima and introduced to their three sons – Nazir, ten years of age, Imtiaz, eight years of age and, Khursheed, who was only three months young then. Their house was a very large Victorian semi-detached property on four floors, unlike the majority of houses in Trafford Park which were terraced. My brother 'Doc's' surgery and waiting room were part of the ground floor of the property. There was an extensive basement which was useful for storage. I was very fortunate to be allocated a spacious attic bedroom for which I was allowed to choose my own decor and furniture. Before my brother Ismail returned to London, my brother 'Doc', Ismail and I had a brief discussion of the educational opportunities that I would need to explore in the near future. The next couple of weeks were spent in exploring my new environment and learning and adjusting to a new life within a totally different social and family setting. This early learning experience included trying to understand my two young nephews and their pronounced Manchester accent. An illustration of my confusion of this was when one of them, before setting off for school, yelled in his heavy Manchester accent 'Moom can I have me jam butties'. Just for a moment I thought I was in a different country but fortunately their mother, my sister-in-law, interpreted this for me and stated that 'they wanted their packed lunch of jam sandwiches'. It is interesting to note that one of the Jam Butties gang became an eminent Professor of Paediatrics and the other carved out a very successful career working as a System Analyst for a multinational company and international banks. How much of their success can be attributed to 'jam butties' I am still not sure of.

Over the next few weeks I gradually adjusted to living in my brother's family home and the abiding memory I have of this period was of the extra-ordinary kindness shown to me by all members of the family and the way they treated me as a member of it. An interesting fact regarding my three young nephews was that each of them was born in a different continent: Nazir was born in South Africa, Imtiaz was born in East Pakistan, and Khursheed was born in England. During this early period of living in Trafford Park I also remember my delight in seeing snow for the first time in my life.

Photograph of me taken in Trafford Park in 1963 in my new environment

My brother 'Doc's' entrance into working as a GP was a circuitous one since his qualifications from Dhaka were only partly recognised in the UK. As a result he had to complete a number of supplementary qualifications and work as Houseman at Whittington Hospital prior to receiving fully registered status as a GP. A medical colleague recommended that he should consider joining a GP practice in Manchester which was seeking a third partner. He joined the partnership and part of the condition was that he would be based in Trafford Park where the practice already had patients. As the newest member of the three partners, he was working long hours not only in the two open surgeries he had on Monday to Friday and Saturday morning but also the numerous 'house visits' he had to undertake on a regular basis. He gradually built up the practice to over a thousand NHS patients as well as an expanding private patients' practice among the Asian and African-Caribbean communities in Old Trafford and beyond. This was a direct result of his honest, non-patronising and caring approach for individual patients.

In contrast, my sister-in-law Halima, having worked in London whilst my brother 'Doc' was completing his registration, was now not only managing a household with one extra person but also caring for baby Khursheed. She had a weekly help, a charming person of Irish descent called Mrs. Finney who lived locally. In brief, I settled quickly into this very busy household and began to take stock of what I needed to consider doing to make personal progress. My brother 'Doc' made an appointment with a neuro-surgeon in Manchester, to review the medical notes and information I brought with me from South Africa and consider the medical/surgical options regarding my right hand. The eminent neuro-surgeon, after conducting the review and meeting 'Doc' and me, informed us that unfortunately the damage to the brain was permanent and that no further surgical treatment was advisable. He also informed me that whilst my hand looked 'normal' now, as I got older, there would be muscle wastage to my right hand. The implication of this was clear to me; that any hope that I entertained of restoring the normal use of my right hand was not possible and that my left hand must be more prominent in my activities and particularly of relearning to write. This also meant that if I wished to make progress in my life, then the educational route was critical and one which had the most possibilities for my future life.

Realising that if I wanted to further my education, I would have to learn to write faster with my left hand. I commenced on this painstaking process of re-learning to write with my left hand: I spent days, weeks and months on this task. Unfortunately I had neglected doing this whilst living in South Africa as I had unrealistic expectation that I would regain the full use of my right hand in the near future. Over the next few months, my handwriting gradually improved but my slow speed of writing was going to be a lifelong feature and a drawback in particular circumstances. The winter months soon passed and after the Easter holidays, I enrolled at Stretford Technical College on their 'O' level course. The prime purpose of enrolling at Easter was for me to get used to both the educational system in England as well as to learn to study again. On reflection, the encouragement to do this by my two brothers was a wise move since it not only allowed me to gradually resume studying again but also assisted me to adjust to an educational environment where almost all the students were 'white' and access to libraries and learning was not based on the colour of your skin. This was a difficult transition, perhaps because the legacy of early conditioning under Apartheid lingered on for a long period of time. During this early period, I was also learning a lot from my young nephews, Nazir and Imtiaz, and I was very grateful for the guidance they provided me on the procedures to enrol at the public library. As an Asian, growing up under Apartheid, we were denied access to libraries. Once enrolled as a borrower, I was delighted to have access to all sorts of reading material and books but the book that brought immediate joy was 'Black Beauty', which we all know is about horses, but was banned by the Apartheid Government in South Africa since they considered it as 'subversive literature'. In return, I also enjoyed taking my young nephews to watch their first Manchester United match playing at Old Trafford. During this period of adjustment, I continued re-learning to write with my left hand.

In the summer of 1962, my childhood friends Cassim Bhabha and his cousin Ahmed paid me a visit in Manchester and brought me up to date with the latest news about family, friends and the growing political unrest and oppression in South Africa. I spent an enjoyable few days with them, including a coach trip to Blackpool. An interesting element of our trip to Blackpool was that my friends sat together on the coach and I sat next to a retired and charming old man. After a brief introduction, he proceeded to tell me his life story and showed me small photographs of his family. The whole journey took around two hours and he continued in this vein. By the end of the journey, it dawned upon me how much loneliness single old people faced in England, in stark contrast to the extended family networks I was brought up with and still enjoy.

In 1963, Blackpool with two South African Friends

Later that year my mother flew in from South Africa for a visit. She brought me up to date with events of the family both from South Africa and Mozambique. Whilst she was with us, my mother and I paid a brief visit to Doctor Mosam's family in Dublin. The Mosams were very good friends from South Africa and besides the Doctor, his two younger nephews were also studying medicine at Dublin University.

Going abroad was one of the ways Asians from South Africa were able to further their aspirations in the field of medicine. After qualifications, many went back to South Africa to practice. It was also a period when my brother Ismail and my sister-in-law, Kaisa became parents with the birth of their son Adam.

At the beginning of September 1962, I enrolled as a full time student at Stretford Technical College studying for five 'O' levels. Most of my contemporaries were seventeen or eighteen years of age and I soon became friends with several of them. I travelled to College normally using two buses – Trafford Park to Old Trafford and then another bus to Stretford Technical College (now it is part of the merged and larger Trafford College). The College was located opposite Old Trafford Cricket Ground. In the warmer weather, friends of mine – Chris, Lynn, Irene and I normally walked to the Old Trafford bus stop – and the two girls frequently argued about who should carry my briefcase. I was bemused by this and did not register the significance of it until much later. Whilst I was making academic progress, my writing was still very slow. This was a particular disadvantage in an age when students had to take notes either from the chalk board or lecturers dictating notes. In some subjects handouts were issued, printed on the 'Banda' machine but this was not common. I was, however, singularly impressed by the very high level of commitment of all the lecturers not only in terms of their knowledge of their respective areas of the curriculum but also the way they supported the students in and out of class. As a slighter older student than my contemporaries, coupled to being able to communicate with my fellow classmates, I was relatively at ease in this new environment. One of the optional subjects we were encouraged to take was with the English Speaking Board. During the first lesson, I recall that the female tutor taking us asked each one of us to say a sentence or two to enable her to gauge our proficiency in the language. When my turn came, I thought that I would use this opportunity to amuse my fellow students and in a very deliberate and "upper class' English voice I recited 'How Now Brown Cow'. Whilst this briefly amused the class, the tutor was surprised/offended and simply stated 'thank you Ahmed and you may wish to know my surname is 'Brown'. That was an embarrassing and salutary lesson for me in terms of classroom etiquette.

Living with my brother and his family in Trafford Park was very comfortable and besides learning to do things independently in terms of my education, I was introduced by 'Doc' to watching wrestling. At certain times of the year, normally on Saturday evenings, 'Doc', Nazir, Imtiaz and I went to 'Belle Vue', an entertainment centre to watch live wrestling. I can still recall such wonderful wrestlers as 'Big Daddy' and 'Giant Haystack' as well as their remarkable choreography skills as they moved and danced across the ring. One of the important aspects of living with my late brother 'Doc' was that he introduced me to regular reading of the Manchester Guardian (now 'The Guardian') and 'The Observer' newspapers. After over fifty years I still take pleasure in regularly reading these informative newspapers. One of the drawbacks of leaving South Africa and living in England was that tropical fruits, so abundant in South

Africa, were not readily available in Manchester in the 1960's. So instead of mangoes, paw paws, passion fruit and others, I was encouraged by 'Doc' to start eating apples and pears. In addition to eating more tropical fruits nowadays, I still try to have my daily apple.

The only hiccup and a major embarrassment, I recall, living with my brother and his family occurred was when I had a surprise visit from a girl student friend called Lynn in late spring of 1963. She called at 'Doc's' house late one afternoon when he was attending his surgery. I was totally surprised by this visit but asked her in to the sitting room. Unfortunately after a few minutes, one of 'Doc's' private patients rang the bell because private patients, instead of attending surgery, came to the main entrance. My nephew let the patient in and she sat with us in the sitting room. After a few minutes of awkward silence, foolishly, I asked Lynn to come upstairs to my bedroom just to talk with some degree of privacy. The magnitude of this simple foolish act on my part has to be gauged against the fact that this was a relatively traditional Moslem household and that to have a girl visitor was bad enough, but to invite her to your bedroom was a 'no-no' in CAPITAL LETTERS. After a few minutes upstairs, my nephew, Nazir knocked on my door and asked me to come down as my brother wished to speak to me. My brother 'Doc', whilst this interrupted his normal surgery, calmly explained to me that this was not acceptable behaviour and pointed out to me that I would not have taken a girl up to my room had I been living in South Africa. I accepted his reasoning and quietly went to my room and explained to Lynn what my brother had said. Then Lynn and I went for a brief walk in Trafford Park. Thinking about it now, I cannot understand why she came to visit me and more importantly what possessed me to ask Lynn to come upstairs to my bedroom? Surprisingly nothing more was said about this very unfortunate incident and our lives return to normality. In due course, I built a very good rapport with the whole family and particularly with my three young nephews and this lasted over fifty years and still continues to this day.

The period after the Whit holidays was my first taste of preparing for my 'O' level exams. Whilst I was reasonably confident of my subjects, my writing was still very slow. This problem of writing slower than my previous capacity to write with my right hand, remained with me all of my life and has militated against me performing better in timed examinations. Even now, I cannot recall having ever satisfactorily completed a timed examination paper at college or at university. Writing slower was not a problem for writing essays and dissertations in my own time and where my grades were consistently better. It was only later in life when I started teaching that I learnt that I could have asked either for an amanuensis (someone to write for me by dictation in a separate facility) or be given extra time to complete the writing. Perhaps I did not bring it to anyone's attention because of the overwhelming desire on my part to be regarded as 'normal' and independent. In my first year of attending college as a full time student, I was very disappointed since I managed to pass only two 'O' levels. During the summer, I continued practising writing with my left hand and was determined to make progress on this front. In the summer, I was encouraged by my brother to take a few driving lessons in order to make myself familiar with driving in the U.K. prior to taking my driving test. This was my second of three driving tests where I have passed at my first attempt, the first one being in South Africa and the last one was in Zambia in the 1970's.

I was very fortunate that the lecturers at Stretford Technical College had more faith in my ability than I did and they encouraged me to enrol on the 'one year three 'A' level course' and re-sit the English O' levels in November 1963. Subsequent events proved that their confidence was not misplaced. In addition to passing the 'O' level, I obtained three reasonably good 'A' level passes plus a good grade in 'The Use of English', which was then an essential qualification to enter university. Whilst I now had the necessary qualifications to go to university, I had not applied that academic year primarily because of self-doubt. Instead I enrolled in September 1964 to study for two more 'A' levels. However, I am jumping ahead of myself because I need to mention that in the autumn of 1963 we all moved to a detached house on Barton Road, Stretford. My late brother's family still own that property and my sister-in-law Halima still lives there. This was a much more comfortable and warmer abode and my good sized bedroom overlooked the rear garden.

Living on Barton Road in Stretford was very convenient and was well placed for access to all major bus routes, social amenities and friends. One of my friends from College, 'Cass' Cassidy, lived just round the corner and he was a regular visitor to the household. Normally when 'Cass' visited us, Nazir, Imtiaz, 'Cass' and I played monopoly. After several of his visits, he remarked that he not only always lost when playing with us but always came out the poorest. We all may have either looked at him with a great degree of compassion or guilt since I made the first confession that the reason I frequently won was because I cheated. 'Cass' was obviously very shocked to learn this but he was mortified when Nazir and Imtiaz also confessed that they also won because they also cheated. After that when 'Cass' visited us, we rarely played monopoly and concentrated our efforts on the card game 'Rummy'. Whilst living on Barton Road, I was asked by my sister-in-law, Halima to 'teach' Nazir and Imtiaz about the Moslem religion once a week. Since my knowledge of this subject was very limited, after the first few weeks, my efforts were directed to talk about politics, social issues and above all, teaching Nazir and Imtiaz several card games. On one of these 'lessons' unfortunately my sister-in-law came into the room with all of us still looking at the cards in our hands. She was understandably shocked by this revelation and I was severely reprimanded. In retrospect, the only saving grace about this is that both Nazir and Imtiaz are still relatively good at playing Monopoly and Rummy.

The event that was most disturbing to all the family in Manchester was to do with my young nephew, Khursheed. For a significant period of time, my sister-in-law, Halima kept bringing to the attention of my brother, 'Doc' that there was something amiss with Khursheed's health, particularly his breathing and at times his facial expressions and colour. Little did

I realise then, the power of maternal instinct. After a number of times of bringing this up with my brother, he consented to a second opinion. Khursheed was diagnosed with a medical condition referred to as an " atrail septal defect " and in laymen's' language " a hole in the heart" and shortly after that he underwent surgery to address the problem. This was the first of his two major operations, the second one occurring when he was seventeen years of age.

During my second year at College I quickly realized that all my full-time contemporaries were equally new to this environment and 'being in the same boat' and sharing many of the same classes, my circle of friends grew. I was very friendly with Chris, a Polish student and we shared a similar outlook on broader political and social issues. He was important in my life as he introducing me to such things as the Manchester Sports Guild for live jazz performances which we attended on either Friday or Saturday evenings. More important than that, he was also instrumental in introducing me to the Manchester section of the Anti Apartheid Movement with its very close links to Manchester University in early 1964. As a relatively recent arrival from South Africa, who was subjected to many of the evils of Apartheid, the existing members quizzed me about how they could demonstrate support for the subjugated people of South Africa? I considered this for a while and suggested that since we were drawing close to the fourth anniversary of the Sharpeville Massacre, a symbolic way to commemorate this, as well as demonstrate support would be by having a torch light procession through Manchester City Centre with 69 mock coffins on Saturday 21 March 1964. The 69 mock coffins were to symbolise the 69 innocent people shot dead by the South African police as well as the hundreds of people shot in the back in Sharpeville, South Africa. The 69 people killed were part of a peaceful protest against the iniquities of the Pass Laws. This was agreed at the meeting, and on the 21 March 1964, we marched through the City Centre with 69 mock coffins and hundreds of torches to show our solidarity with the oppressed peoples of South Africa. The Manchester University students, who were members of Anti Apartheid movement, did a magnificent job constructing the 69 mock coffins and producing a multitude of torches. This was my introduction to the politics of protest and a timely reminder that I must not ever forget the struggles of my friends, family and the peoples of South Africa against the evils of Apartheid.

As previously mentioned, my second year at College was successful and I was encouraged by my tutors to apply for a university place. In the 1960's, university applicants had to complete a form indicating six choices in order of preference. Normally, the first three choices would offer you an interview and possibly an offer subject to certain conditions such as particular pass grades. My first three choices, Sheffield, Manchester and Hull, all offered me a place. I was impressed by the lecturers who interviewed at Hull University and made that my first choice. I was given a conditional offer from Hull on passing one further 'A' Level examination at a particular grade. At the end of the college academic year, I passed the examination with one grade higher than the conditional offer. My last year at Stretford Technical College was less stressful than my first two years for reasons outlined previously. This more relaxed environment allowed me to further develop my friendships with my contemporaries.

I still vividly recall several incidents from those days. One of my friends, John, was very approachable and trusting and he was looking for a girl friend. Being aware of this, I took out an attractive photograph of a girl, called Krystina, from my wallet and persuaded John that I was no longer interested in her since I wished to 'go out' with her sister and Krystina may be interested in a new boy friend. John was very interested in this possibility and enquired about how he should go about this. I pulled out from my pocket a phone number and suggested to him to ring this number and ask for a Miss Lion. At lunch time, he found the courage to phone the number I gave him and asked to speak to Miss Lion. The person at the other end of the phone informed John that his was the second phone call he had received that day asking to speak to Miss Lion. Furthermore, he informed John that the number he called was Belle Vue Zoo and that did he realise that that day was the 1st April. For the rest of that academic year, John was very cautious of accepting anything I said as reliable.

Not long after that an equally amusing episode occurred when Peter, another friend from college, and I were in Manchester and he stated that 'today is my grandfather's birthday and since he has a good sense of humour, I want to play a joke on him as well as wish him a happy birthday on the phone'. He asked me to speak to him since he would not recognise my voice. Peter phoned his grandfather and I spoke to him in the best Indian accent I could muster and informed him that I was representing a particular Asian Embassy and that he was the lucky winner of our annual surprise birthday prize. For a short period he sounded to be pleased and enquired about the nature of the prize. I informed him, in my best Indian accent, that the prize was a fully grown live elephant. He was obviously taken aback by this information and begun to give reason why he did not want the prize. When I suggested to him that the prize was already on its way to him, he stated that he did not have the appropriate food to feed an elephant. My reply was that in addition to the lorry bringing the elephant, there was a second lorry following it with all the appropriate food to last a month and that every month he would receive a free supply of this food as long as the elephant was alive. At that stage, I hastily wished him the best of luck with his prize and concluded the phone call. About five minutes later Peter phoned him up and wished him a happy birthday and informed him of the joke and his grandfather replied that he really thought an elephant was on its way to him but quickly realised that someone was playing a joke on him.

An incident at the time which surprised me was when a friend from college called Tony and I went to watch a cricket Test Match at Old Trafford Cricket Ground, which was opposite Stretford Technical College. During the lunch break, I brought out a couple of oranges and offered Tony one. He looked at me embarrassed and bewildered about 'how he should go about eating it'. He was from a single parent family as his father died during the war and fruits such as an orange were outside his sphere of experience. Growing up in South Africa, where fruit was in abundant supply, I was very surprised to learn that some fruits were not as readily available to many people in post-war Britain. Another illuminating incident regarding Tony was when I was asked by a Greek Cypriot friend, Nicolas, what did it mean when Tony told him to 'belt up'? I was fortunate in that I was aware of the colloquial use of the English language which many foreign students found difficult to comprehend. Idioms and metaphors such as 'belt up', 'kicking the bucket', 'get off your soap box', etc. meant very little to them. I was also aware that Tony and Nicolas had frequently indulged in heated arguments about a variety of political issues, and in order to avoid a fight between them, I had to use my best diplomatic skills. I informed Nicolas that 'belt up' simply refers to asking him to 'keep quiet but a little stronger'. This appeared to satisfy him and he just walked away. Early in my third year attending College, I was introduced by a friend to a girl named Rita and we became 'romantically attached'. She was from a Roman Catholic background and was very keen to pursue our relationship despite the fact she was intending to go to London to train as a nurse, and I intended to go to Hull to pursue a course in higher education. On one of our outings, she surprised me and stated that if I wished to marry her, her family would only accept me if/when I converted and become a Roman Catholic. My instant reply to her was 'I have no trouble in converting to become a Roman Catholic, but by the same token, my family would only accept you if you converted and become a Moslem'. The romantic relationship did not last much after that. Moreover, I was then more concerned about preparing to go to university than in marriage.

The abiding memory of my first three and half years in England was of the extraordinary kindness and concern for my educational progress and personal well being shown to me by my two brothers and their respective families. My two brothers clearly demonstrated to me that by setting realistic goals and through hard graft, much can be achieved both personally and professionally.

CHAPTER FOUR

HIGHER EDUCATION

At the end of Sept 1965, having secured the necessary A levels to go to University to read Economics and Economic and Social History, I packed my large trunk, which I originally brought from South Africa, with clothes, books and papers which I assumed I would need at University. A friend of the family drove me in his van to the university owned semi-detached student house on Cranbrook Avenue, Hull. On arrival, I was welcomed by Peter, the senior student at the house. Besides Peter who was completing his PHD in Geography, I shared the house with 5 other students – two students named David, both studying Law who shared a double bedroom, Robin who was studying Philosophy and Alan who was studying Literature, all in their final year. Whilst at the starting of the term I had a large double bedroom by myself, later in the term Peter Jones, another first year student, joined me in my room and we shared the double room for the year: he was also reading Economics. After the Fresher's week I quickly settled in to the role of student life including lectures, tutorials and going to social and political events. Some of the benefits of going to Hull were that living independently, away from home for the first time was both interesting and rewarding as I had to learn new skills such as cooking, laundering, cleaning and so on. These lifelong skills were acquired gradually at university in my first year.

One of the more amusing episode of sharing a house with final year students made up of two lawyers, one philosopher, one literature specialist and a geographer was one evening when I asked them to solve a problem, which I had been mulling over for some time, since they individually and collectively possessed far greater expertise than me. The problem I posed to them was as follows: 'Let us assume that we are neighbours and I possess a peacock; the peacock is living relatively free in my garden; one day the peacock jumps over the fence into your garden and lays an egg. The question is who does this egg belong to?' As they began to consider this, Peter, my roommate and I left to go to the student union building for a coffee. We returned to our student house after two hours, and to our astonishment, they were still discussing the question about the ownership of the egg. They asked me if I had the answer to this question since they could not agree on the ownership of the egg. I explained to them that the answer was relatively simple: 'Look at the question and consider whether it is logically possible for a peacock to lay an egg? It is peahens that lay eggs not peacocks.' At this point Peter and I made a hasty retreat to our room and locked the door to prevent a lynching.

In my second term at University, Peter, the Geographer and I agreed to jointly purchase a second hand car for £45 – a Ford Prefect. The purchase of the car was both for our personal use and for Peter to learn to drive. As I was already a qualified driver,

I taught Peter to drive for a period of time and he subsequently went to the driving school to finish off his driving skills. After he had passed his test, I acquired Peter's share of the car and this was the first car I owned. There were several interesting features to this car: besides having a 'running board' it also had a front window which opened a few inches as well as two indicator arms with an orange light. The indicator arms were not only useful to indicate turning, but when parked they were also proved useful to wave at 'good looking' girls passing by. The car was also useful to go back to Manchester during the vacation periods – a long drive as then the M62 did not exist.

During the 2nd term, I also began to realise that besides the academic life there was also a political and social life at the university. In the course of this term, I began a friendship with David Collins who also lived on Cranbrook Avenue in another of the university's houses. We shared a similar outlook to social and political issues as well as doing an identical range of courses. Even at this early part of our university life, we began to attend political society meetings together. He also assisted me in reviving the Anti-Apartheid Movement at the university. At the beginning of the last term, David and I agreed to share a rented flat. Our search eventually led us to an unfurnished flat on Coltman Street in Hull -the street was reputed to be in the red light district but I'm not sure of that. The unfurnished, poorly decorated flat was approximately four miles from the university and having a car was extremely useful, particularly in bad weather. We agreed to rent this upstairs flat which comprised two bedrooms, a bathroom and a landing with a miniscule kitchen. The rent was 'extraordinarily high' at £3 a week.

Once all the university students completed their respective examinations, we were all engaged in preparing for 'Rag Week' which entailed activities associated with raising money for a variety of charities. My final year flat mates were well organised for this and besides the normal collection of money in the shopping area of town, they also decided that we could raise some money from the university seniors. They proposed that we kidnap the skeleton from the senior common room and hold it for ransom. My role in this was to drive the skeleton to a safe hiding place. The kidnapping of the skeleton was successful but no senior staff were willing to 'cough up' the small ransom demanded for the return of the skeleton. After a few days, we realised that they were very unlikely to pay up and consequently we agreed to return the skeleton. We, however, decided that the skeleton had to be returned anonymously so agreed to hang the skeleton, from its neck , on a small road bridge going into town thus ensuring some additional publicity for the 'Rag Week'. We phoned the senior common room with this information and the skeleton was eventually rescued. On a more practical level, Dave Collins and I agreed to move to our flat in late August of 1966 as I had planned to go to Poland in July.

I failed to mention previously that whilst I was at college in Manchester, I continued to correspond with Krystina my pen friend, with whom I first established contact in South Africa. Late in the last term, I accepted Krystina's invitation to visit her and her family in Wroclaw, Poland during the summer vacation. Before

I embarked on the journey to Poland, I spent a few days with my brother Ismail and his family in West Norwood, London. This gave me the opportunity to get to know my young nephew, Adam, better as well as being informed by my sister-in-law Kaisa, of the finer points about visiting Poland. The train journey to Poznan in Poland was peaceful and easy. Then I had to change trains and having no linguistic knowledge or skills in Polish, I blundered my way to Wroclaw. Arriving there was one thing but then I had to negotiate with a taxi driver to take me to the suburb where Krystina and her family lived. I arrived at the house and was welcomed by Krystina's mother. She obviously sensed that the journey was exhausting and she showed me to a bedroom and indicated in easy sign language that I should have a rest. Having slept for a few hours, my first glimpse of Krystina was her sitting in a chair and anxiously waiting for me to wake up. My first impression of Krystina was that she was pleased to see me and she was as good looking as her photograph which I possessed. After a few moments of cleaning up, and before sitting down for a meal, I was introduced to her family – her father, mother, elder sister and young nephew.

During my three weeks visit to Poland, I began to get acquainted with Krystina and her family. I learnt that Krystina was at university studying European Literature and Russian. My only means of communication with Krystina's family was for her to act as a translator. I learnt that her elder sister was previously a pianist with the Polish State Orchestra and that during a trip to West Germany, her husband absconded and left the orchestra and sought and was given political asylum in West Germany. The orchestra was then summoned to return to Poland immediately and Krystina's sister was then both distressed and under suspicion of the then Communist regime. For several years after this event, she refused to play the piano again until she consented to play a piece from Chopin, for her sister's friend from England. I was both humbled and honoured by this moving and wonderful gesture.

Krystina was very astute and organised a busy schedule of visits for both of us to visit throughout Poland. This not only provided me with a rare opportunity to visit places in Poland with an articulate and well informed guide but also offered us the opportunity to get to know each other better. Our travel arrangement for visiting different parts of Poland necessitated Krystina obtaining a permit from the appropriate authorities. My understanding of this was that there was no cost involved but it was a requirement for people living in Poland at the time. I was thus surprised to see Krystina attaching a 20 Zlotys note under the application form for the permit. After we obtained the necessary permit, I enquired of Krystina of 'why did you pay 20 Zlotys for something that was free?' Her reply was illuminating and she stated that if we wish to make the trip in the next few days, that was considered a normal way things work in Poland and that if she did not pay, her application would be lingering at the bottom of the pile for weeks and weeks.

The first place we travelled by train to was to the north coastal resort of Hel. We were there for a few days and I could not resist the temptation to send friends and family postcards with comments such as

'Hell is not such a bad place after all', 'I am going to Hell', and 'I have been to Hell and back'. The other memorable visits I made with Krystina were to the mountain region of 'Zakopane', the beautiful old city of Krakow, the salt mine where I was amazed by the beautiful salt crystal engraving of the Last Supper, other engravings and the wonderful chandeliers created with salt crystals. The place, however, which overwhelmed me was our visit to Auschwitz, the German prisoner of war camp. We planned a whole day visit here but three hours after commencing the visit and witnessing, through the exhibits, some of the most barbaric acts men committed against fellow human beings, I was shocked and could no longer continue. We spent the rest of the day drinking coffee in a cafe and talking about what we had witnessed and we felt saddened by the fact that some of those atrocities were still prevalent in different parts of the world. Shortly after this traumatic visit, we returned to Wroclaw and I invited Krystina to visit me in England in the summer of 1967.

Shortly after the visit to Poland, I returned to Hull. In

Krystina, her nephew and me in regional costumes

addition to cleaning the flat, we also had to furnish it since the only item that the landlord provided was an old electric cooker, Dave and I set about the task of organising our flat. I was very fortunate in that I purchased a bedroom suite (minus a mattress) from a 'Rag & Bone' man wheeling these items on a cart in Coltman Street for the princely sum of 30 shillings (£1.50 in today's money). This comprised of a double bed frame, a wardrobe and a marble wash stand including a jug and bowl. I then began painting this wonderful furniture light mauve and pale yellow, bought a mattress and the necessary bedding and was set for the next two years in terms of sleeping quarters. I was more confident with commencing year two of my university course than year one. Sometime in September 1966, Dave and I began living in our flat making rapid adjustments for peacefully sharing the accommodation. In our early discussions about sharing the daily meals, Dave informed me that he was not good at this task and would appreciate it if I did the cooking and he would assist with this. In our discussions about food, Dave came up with a suggestion, which at the time was eminently sensible, and that was to purchase from wholesalers boxes of tinned pilchards, since the fish was very rich in nutrients and relatively cheap. A couple of boxes of tinned pilchards were purchased and my task was to use these in cooking. For the next couple of weeks, I used the limited culinary skills I possessed to creatively use tinned pilchards: we began eating pilchards casserole, pilchards risotto, pilchards pie, curried pilchards with rice, pilchards pizzas, pilchards on toast, pilchards sandwiches, pilchards with baked potatoes and simply pilchards with bread. Whilst we did consume other meals as well, the staple diet was tinned pilchards. After a couple of weeks of this experiment in catering, we both came to the same conclusion that the wholesale purchase of tinned pilchards was no longer necessary. This also had a long term effect on my future eating habits since I developed a pathological dislike of tinned pilchards for a considerable time. The other absurd idea we embarked upon involved the bath tub. The metal bath tub was in a very poor condition regarding the surface and we agreed to improve it by painting it with enamel paint. After some discussion, we agreed that the colour needed to be a warm and comforting colour and we decided to paint the bath tub RED. Whilst in theory, the choice was a reasonable one, we discovered several problems after the painting of the bath tub was completed. Firstly, it took an inordinately long time for the paint to dry and therefore it was out of commission for a couple of weeks and secondly, even after several weeks , every time we had a bath, we ended up with red bottoms. Eventually, the bath tub was dry and all the flaking paint was bodily removed by Dave's and my bottom.

As I personally grew more confident in my second year at university, and with support from Dave Collins, I began to explore the political and social environment of the different student societies. I was encouraged by Janet Blackman, a senior lecturer at the university, to join the United Nations Student Association at the university. Very shortly after I joined, it dawned on me that this could be a very useful vehicle to initiate something totally different from the normal discussions and of inviting guest speakers on current international issues. I slowly commenced to take a leading role in the Association by proposing and organising an international children's art exhibition. I proposed that we invite children, five to eleven years of age, from all over the world to submit paintings on at least one of three specific themes – their environment, transport and nature. Dave and a number of fellow students assisted me with this massive task. We wrote to the different foreign embassies in London inviting their respective education ministries and schools to submit their paintings for this exhibition. This international children's art exhibition, possibly the first in the world, had a very favourable response from nearly forty countries from all five continents. The task of coordinating and presenting several hundred paintings was both daunting and rewarding. The Exhibition was hosted by the Hull City Art Gallery and was attended by a significant number of school parties from Hull and the surrounding district as well as members of the public. The brochure for the exhibition included a contribution from an eminent child psychologist who made a variety of astute comments about the way children see their respective environments but she also noted that the choice and use of colours by children differed significantly between those from the colder temperate climate countries and those children who lived in warmer regions.

After a few weeks, the art exhibition moved to a stately home in Beverly. In addition to initiating and helping to organise the art exhibition, I was also busy with organising activities of the Anti-Apartheid Movement and particularly the boycott of South African products including 'Outspan' oranges. Whilst we realised that the economic impact of this protest was small, as someone who experience the iniquities of apartheid, I argued that it was an important symbolic gesture for fellow sufferers in South Africa to be assured that their struggle was not forgotten by people in England. I was also acutely aware that the South African Apartheid Government 'planted' white South African informers at various universities in England. At one of the parties held in our flat in Coltman Street, I stumbled on a white South African called John P, who was alone in my bedroom searching through my book collection and papers. I confronted him and he made some lame excuse about whether I had some good South African novels for him to read. During this period, I was also involved in the CND movement and with Dave participated in the Aldermaston march. In my spare time, I studied – just joking. In retrospect, the second year at university was full of extra-curricular activities as well as a busy academic life. An interesting part of studying for an economics degree was that we also had to complete an additional course in Statistics. This course was interestingly delivered to over a hundred students by a well qualified lecturer whose only minor problem in delivery was the repeated use of the phrase 'so as to speak'. Several colleagues and I decided that we needed to put our statistical education to the test. We plotted on a graph the frequency of the use of the phrase 'so as to speak' used by this lecturer as well as the pattern of preceding the use of this phrase in lectures. We then tested this and recorded on paper how this occurred. We then agreed that in future, before he used this phrase, several of us would simultaneously shout out the phrase 'so as to speak'. Whilst the lecturer and fellow students were shocked by our behaviour, at the end of the term, the lecturer came to inform us that whilst he was initially annoyed at our regular interruptions of calling out loudly 'so as to speak', he thanked us for bringing this to his attention and also for applying a statistical method in doing this. He informed us that he was now fully cured of this affliction 'so as to speak'.

Once the summer vacation commenced, I began preparing for the arrival of Krystina from Poland. She arrived in late July and after a few days in London, we departed for Manchester. We stayed with a university friend and his girl friend and we all agreed to meet again in a few days time in St. Ives, Cornwall. Whilst we were in Manchester, we visited a variety of local places of interest including the Lake District. Krystina and I developed a romantic relationship in this period. We spent the last week of Krystina's vacation in Hull and agreed that we would like to take our relationship further and possibly get married in the near future. We planned on getting married after both of us had completed our university courses . I also agreed to visit Poland during the winter vacation – December 1967/January 1968.

At the start of my final year at the University of Hull, little did I realise that this was going to be such an intensive and momentous year not only the academic sense but also on the personal front. In September, there were new tenants in the downstairs flat: Fred, a mathematics lecturer at the university and his girl friend, Marge (later to become his wife) moved into the large double bedroom and a friend of theirs, Jane moved into the other bedroom. Jane, at the time was 'going out' with a friend of mine. After an academically demanding first term, I commenced my visit to Poland. The travel arrangement were very unusual – I took a flight from London to Berlin, West Germany then planned to take a train from Berlin in East Germany to Wroclaw. After an unplanned night in B&B in West Berlin, I obtained a visa and went through 'Check Point Charlie' into East Germany. The train ride through East Germany in winter was interesting and much of the train was occupied by soldiers returning home for Christmas. The soldiers were obviously curious about me and endeavoured to have a conversation with me in English and much of their emphasis was on swapping my western clothes with their winter coats ,etc. No trade took place and I arrived in Wroclaw in good spirit and prepared for the sub-zero temperatures, which were normal for that time of the year. While the Christmas celebration was enjoyable with exchanging of appropriate gifts and meals, Krystina arranged for New Year celebrations for the two of us at an expensive restaurant, with a seven course dinner. We were now unofficially engaged (with the blessing of her family) and much of the time together centred round Krystina coming to England and us getting married. It was very apparent to me that Krystina was very enthusiastic to leave Communist Poland with all the constraints that she perceived the regime placed on her life. My planned departure from Wroclaw to England was during a very bad snow storm. I planned to take a train to the northern sea port of Gdynia and then take the cargo boat, previously booked, from there to Hull. Unfortunately no trains were running and there was no flight either. Eventually the two of us plus another person who wished to go to Gdynia hired a taxi to take us there. The trip of several hundred miles through a major snow storm in a Russian built Volga car was a memorable journey. Once we arrived at the port, I boarded the cargo vessel going to Hull, as the only passenger. Leaving the port and going through the Kiel Canal was a relatively pleasant experience and as the only passenger, I was privileged to have my first wonderful meal with the Captain. Then we 'hit' the North Sea and it was exceptionally rough. This was a period when severe storms hit the North Sea and it was also during this period when several large fishing vessels were lost at sea. At this point, I confined myself to my cabin, felt nauseated and no longer wished to be fed. I only emerged from my cabin, two days later as we approached the calmer waters of the Humber. Waiting at the dockside were my flat mates including Dave Collins and Jane Hibberd from the downstairs flat. They were pleased to see me but amused by my 'pale' complexion and Cossack hat.

In January 1968, the Apartheid regime in South Africa was still administering its inhumane system of segregation and discrimination and I decided to apply for British citizenship instead of going back to South Africa. The pressure of academic life was building up in my final year but the weekends were still a time for relaxing with friends. On one such weekend late in the term, Jane had some friends from Cambridge visiting her and we all agreed to go to a disco in York by car. We enjoyed the evening and on the way back, a friend volunteered to drive my car back and I sat with two of the girls at the back. Jane was in the rear seat next to me and on the way back, her body language, suggested that she was interested in forming a romantic relationship with me. Whilst I was surprised, my response was unambiguous and positive to her overtures. The relationship began to grow over several weeks and transformed into an intensive romantic relationship, during my final term of my final year at university. I then had to face several deeply troublesome issues regarding my future life, not only preparing for my finals but on the personal front about informing Krystina about this dramatic change of circumstances and that I no longer wished to marry her. I realised that this would be a devastating blow to her but the alternative of living a lie was not in my nature. This, at the time, was one of the most agonising and difficult letters I had to write. For weeks after posting it, I felt very guilty and uneasy. As the final term progressed, I had to determine my future career plans and decided to apply to one of the Technical Teachers College, affiliated to an appropriate university, to study for a post graduate certificate in education – a PGCE. Whilst in my final term, I was accepted by Wolverhampton Technical Teachers' College, at that time affiliated to Birmingham University. In late June, after completing my finals, I received a letter confirming my naturalisation as a British citizen.

In late June, I met Jane's parents, Mr. and Mrs.

Hibberd and informed them of Jane's and my wish to get married. They were surprised at the suddenness of our decision, and after some discussion about our future plans, they were supportive. I failed to mention previously, that Jane was reading English Literature at University and during her first year, she had to abandon her studies as she suffered a major brain aneurism and was hospitalised for a period. When we met, she was repeating her first year of the course. Our decision to get married resulted in Jane temporarily giving up her course and moving with me to the Midlands for one year. On the 15th July, 1968 Jane I got married at the Cambridge Registrars Office and enjoyed a wonderful reception in Granchester, Cambridge. Among the guest I invited, besides close members of my family, Dave Collins 'Best Man', several university and college friends, there was my friend and neighbour from South Africa – Ahmed Timol. Ahmed Timol and I met several times in London where he was working for a short while. I will elaborate on this later since his life had a profound effect on my political values and beliefs. After we were married, Jane and I left for a couple of days in Oxford and then to Edinburgh to stay in Anne's, Jane's sister's, flat for a week. I realised then, that was the end of 'one chapter' of my life and the beginning of another.

The three years I spent in Hull obviously had a profound influence on my subsequent life. I completed my university education, which was a very distant dream when I was living in South Africa. I also realised that with effort and commitment, many things professionally were possible plus I fell in love and married Jane. I was very fortunate to have met a friend for life in Dave Collins, who was very supportive over the two years we shared a flat. We spent many hours in each other's company but I cannot recall ever falling out with him. Whilst we shared many political activities, his support in assisting me to organise the first International Children's Art Exhibition was invaluable.

CHAPTER FIVE

THE JOY OF LEARNING AND TEACHING

There were two urgent tasks which needed attention as soon as Jane and I returned from Edinburgh – firstly, we had to find temporary accommodation for one year while I completed my PGCE course and secondly, I had to make an application for an educational grant to support us for one year. The latter task was new to me as previously, with help from my family, I paid for my college and university education fees and living expenses. In the autumn of 1968, we decided that living in Wolverhampton itself may not be advisable especially given that Enoch Powell's speech regarding immigrants and his reference to 'rivers of blood' was still resonating in the Midlands and beyond and especially as his constituency of Smethwick was close by. We eventually found a very old cottage in the centre of the village/ market town of Shifnal, about 12 miles from Wolverhampton. In early autumn, the furnished cottage appeared as an idyllic starting point for a newly married couple. Its quaint stone floors, a coal fireplace for heating and beamed ceilings added ambience to the place. Once we paid our rent in advance, filled petrol in our small Austin A30 car and purchased essential household items, we realised that between us we possessed thirty shillings (£1.50) to last us for ten days, that is, until my educational grant came in. Whilst we were aware that either of our families would assist us if we asked, we wished to be independent as newlyweds. Thus for a short while, baked potatoes with an assortment of cheap fillings was our staple diet.

The theoretical part of my teacher training course was interesting but the teaching practice at a local college was demanding and enjoyable when things went smoothly. There are two episodes of my teaching practice I recall clearly: the first was when I was being assessed and observed by a senior lecturer, teaching economics to a very helpful cohort of students – the students were trying to be helpful by shouting out answers to questions before I completed writing the questions on the chalk board. Fortunately, this assessment was suddenly brought to a halt when some emergency building work commenced outside the window and the noise from the pneumatic drill was loud enough for that lesson to be abandoned for a later date. The second episode was also when I was being assessed but this time by the head of teaching training department of Wolverhampton Technical Teachers College. The assessment visits occurred with no prior notice and for this particular lesson, I was tasked to help improve the vocabulary of second year mining apprentices. For this particular lesson, with Jane's help, I constructed on a piece of large card a crossword puzzle and divided the class into two teams competing against each other to score more points. As the two teams competed by solving the clues, the Head who was observing me got very excited and kept moving his chair from the back of the class to almost the front. The lesson was graded as 'Excellent' and the following week when all the PGCE students returned to Wolverhampton, the other lecturers informed me that the Head of the College was very complimentary about my teaching skills. This pure chance and unpredictable event reinforced the old idiom that always prepare well for all lessons you deliver to students and expect the unexpected.

We enjoyed the first few months of living in this quaint old cottage when the weather was relatively warm. Once the weather began to change, we realised and experienced the downside of living with stone floors and inadequate heating. The kitchen area was particularly cold with cold draughts coming in from poorly fitted doors and windows. This was brought home to us when bowls of water left overnight in the kitchen froze by the morning. Whilst we adapted to this by buying extra heating appliances the house was still very cold and Jane, when she was not working, spent much of her daytime hours in the laundrette with a book to keep warm. Jane worked over the Christmas period in a department store in Wolverhampton and subsequently as a 'house mother' at a local residential school. The coldness of the cottage was even worse for visitors When my sister, her first husband, and a doctor friend and his wife came to stay with us for a few days in March, they huddled around the coal fire, with an electric heater and a paraffin heater at full blast, still in their overcoats. It was obvious to us that they were feeling very cold and the only explanation we agreed on is that coming to visit us from their holiday in the heat of the Middle East, they did not have time to acclimatise to this very cold cottage. They survived but were pleased to return to my brother's warm house in Manchester. I then began to apply for a teaching post in colleges and was offered an Assistant Lecturer post at Kirby College in Middlesborough.

I accepted the post of Assistant Lecturer in Business Studies at Kirby College, Middlesborough commencing 1st September 1969. The College Principal, Graham Edwards, was an astute and enterprising person who developed the College and extended the range of opportunities for local people in a relatively short time. Prior to the interview, the limited research I completed about the locality indicated that it was a relatively new town heavily dependent on two very large industries nearby – ICI (chemicals) and British Steel. The town was also in close proximity to the seaside resorts of Redcar and Saltburn. The college was a relatively new college based in an old secondary school, located in the suburb of Linthorpe, approximately three miles from the town centre. Jane and I were fortunate in renting a property, within walking distance of the college, for six months. Jane's had a small legacy which enabled us to pay the deposit on our first property on Bentinck Avenue, Linthorpe. We moved into the property with a bed and a small coffee table, a gift from my brother Mahmood. This modern detached house was a short walking distance of the college and we gradually furnished it. We spent the next four and a half happy years in this house. Little did I realise then that Jane's father, George Hibberd, would feature in my life as a professional role model as I progressed in my career. He was a man of total integrity who placed 'student learning' as the guiding principle in managerial decision making.

I am certain that almost all teachers and lecturers entering the education sector will testify that the first year or two are the most demanding and busy in their respective careers. Preparing teaching plans and lesson preparations frequently necessitated burning midnight oil and consuming parts of the weekend. This was essential if you wished to stay several lessons ahead of your students and this task was critical in a relatively small college where almost all lecturers were expected to teach several related subjects instead of only one subject. This was the situation I faced in September and my first major concern on receiving my teaching timetable was trying to decipher and translate the abbreviated notations on it. I was able to work out most of it and was relatively confident that I would be able to deliver the lectures with sufficient preparation. There was one very disturbing abbreviation – I was to teach 'Business and Management Studies 'to a 'PHD' class. I was surprised by this having just recently graduated, I felt that to teach a group of people studying for a Doctorate was way above my ability. With great anxiety, I took my timetable to the Head of the Business Studies Department for clarification. I was immensely relieved when he stated that the 'PHD' on the timetable was an abbreviation for a group of 'Part time Hair Dressing' students and not post graduate students and my remit was to teach them the principles of how a good business should be organised and run. He also informed me that most of the students were about 18 years or older and they were all trainee hairdressers and this was their second year at college.

As a new lecturer, I was advised by the experienced lecturers that some of the older students, who became aware of a beginner, may create a situation by which I may be embarrassed. They further advised me to be aware of this, 'think on your feet', adapt, focus on the perpetrator not the whole class and never lose control of the class. The first situation which potentially could have been problematic, came early in my first term when I was teaching my 'PHD' class business studies: one of the female hairdressing students, without any warning, asked me 'how was your sex life Mr Choonara?' Just for a moment, I was taken aback by this brazen and potentially embarrassing situation, but remembered the wise advice given to me by my senior colleagues, and I asked this same students 'have you any suggestions to make it more interesting?' She was totally embarrassed by this and the rest of the class smiled at this quick response and for the rest of the year, the behaviour of the class was exemplary.

In the same vein, a potentially difficult situation arose later when I was teaching 'Business Studies' to a group of secretarial students. The classroom, in which this lesson was scheduled, was in a flexible typing room where the large desks housed typewriters which were concealed when the lids came down. The lesson was timetabled immediately after the morning 'tea break'. Upon entering the class I found, to my surprise, that there was only one student, Angela present and I enquired about the other fifteen students who were absent. Angela replied that she thought that they were still in the 'concourse' where they had their tea break. As I indicated earlier, the classroom furniture was made up of eighteen large desks and as I considered Angela's reply, I spotted some feet under a couple of desks and realised that all the other students were hiding under the desks. Just for a moment, I considered the options and then proceeded teaching, initially informing Angela that the other students would have to copy her notes from her when she saw them. An hour later, at the end of the lecture, I informed all the students, who sat quietly for an hour in possibly the most uncomfortable position in the classroom, that they needed to emerge from under the desks and loudly stated 'April Fool to you' and that there would be a test on the subject of the lecture the following week. To my surprise, all the students performed above average in the test the following week. Unfortunately, this was a teaching method I was not able to use in my subsequent teaching career.

One of the most profound impacts on my teaching career occurred when I was teaching an evening adult class, 'O' Level Economic and Social History. The topic I was then exploring with the students, one evening, was the development of the textile industries in the early nineteenth century and some of the economic and social issues that accompanied it. I raised the issue that one method that some mill owners used to pay their employees weekly was the 'truck system' – which meant that the employees were paid in particular tokens, instead of money, and these tokens could only be exchanged for goods in the mill owner's shop. One of the students, Graham, put up his hand and informed me that he was an owner of some of these historical tokens. Graham was an adult student in his early twenties and experienced great difficulties in reading and writing – this was long before dyslexia was recognised as a specific learning difficulty. I asked Graham if he would consider bringing these tokens to the class the following week and showing them and speaking for a few minutes about his collection.

The following week, Graham brought these tokens and began nervously showing the adult class the tokens and then, as he grew in confidence, describing, in detail, how they differed, the metals that were used to produce them and their respective values. He had me and the rest of the class spellbound for over half an hour with the depth of his knowledge and the obvious passion with which he collected not only these historical tokens but his collecting of coins generally. As I stated earlier, Graham was a student who was experiencing difficulties in reading and writing but his knowledge and explanation of the 'tokens' was not only very illuminating but also clearly demonstrated to me that in addition to teaching your specialist subject, one of the task of a teacher is to locate and develop the special abilities and passions students possess and not look only at the difficulties and disabilities people experience. In brief, 'look at people's abilities and capabilities and do not over focus on their disabilities'. At the end of this class, I thanked Graham for his important contribution and enquired what he did for a living – he informed me that he was a coin collector and dealer and that he spent much of his time travelling and buying and selling coins between different European countries because the values of different coins differed greatly between countries. He also informed me of what he was earning on average – this was more than double my salary as a lecturer. In brief, he was very successful in what he did to earn a living but critically for me, was the important insight about teaching and learning and that I must never make assumptions about people's ability and instead always explore their capabilities and strengths. Incidentally, despite his personal difficulties, Graham managed to pass his 'O' Level course. In the meantime Jane was working full time for the local health authority in an administrative role. After a few months in this post, she was interviewed and appointed to a more challenging job as a Research Assistant for the Medical Officer of Health for Teesside. An important feature of our marriage was that, in a number of important ways such as scrutinising my application forms and letters, Jane was always very supportive and helpful as my career in further education progressed. Sometime early in 1970 Jane informed me that she was pregnant and that the due date was early in December, 1970. After satisfactorily completing my probationary year as an Assistant Lecturer, I was then appointed as a Lecturer 1 in Business Studies. In September of 1970 I was not only teaching Business Studies but also began teaching General/Liberal Studies to a range of young full time students. This was an interesting opportunity for lecturers to explore a variety of issues with full time students, frequently with external professional experts, ranging from personal health, local environmental issues, and political, legal and social issues as well as giving students an opportunity to participate in a variety of sports. This allowed students to develop, not only academically, but also acquire other important living and coping skills in a rapidly changing environment. In later years sadly this option, allowing young learners to develop a wider perspective of the society they lived in, was abandoned in favour of greater emphasis in developing vocational skills.

Early on 6th December 1970, I drove Jane to the local Maternity Hospital as she was in the early stages of labour. Unfortunately the contractions continued for most of the day and my wish to be present for the birth of our first child was abandoned when later in the evening the hospital staff advised me to go home. Jane was obviously in much discomfort and the process of giving birth, we later learnt, was unnecessarily prolonged. At the time, little did we realise that this protracted labour would have a long term effect on Amy, who was born on the 7th December 1970. In these early years of our life together, we were pleased to be young parents and enjoyed the privilege.

I began to be more confident in my professional life and this allowed me to explore a variety of pedagogic issues such as placing secretarial students for work experience in Children's Homes as part of their Liberal Studies options. This was long before work placement for full time students was introduced. One pleasing outcome of placing students in different work situations was that it not only gave them an understanding of other people's lives but also provided them with an alternative career opportunity, which several students took. I continued to enjoy teaching and learning in my second year at Kirby College.

At the beginning of my third year of teaching in September 1971, little did I realise that this was going to be a momentous year in many ways.

The tragic events in South Africa which occurred in October 1971 (which I cover extensively in the next chapter) made me acutely aware of the fact that I was fortunate in living in a political and legal environment in Great Britain which allowed me to pursue my professional ambitions without fear. During this academic year in addition to teaching economics and business studies, I was taking a much more active role in the teaching of Liberal Studies. Liberal Studies was organised on the basis of allowing students to make a balanced choice, from a variety of options, for one afternoon a week. These options range from difficult political social, legal and environmental issues to drama, music, participation in sports, recreation and arts and craft. This allowed young people to participate in new activities as well encouraging them to explore difficult issues in a non threatening way and develop their understanding of the world they lived in. It also allowed them to explore and participate in sports and recreation. During that academic year, I applied for and was promoted to post as Lecturer Two with responsibility for the Liberal Studies programme for a significant part of the college. This opportunity allowed me to invite specialists from a variety of professions to discuss specific issues with young people in a safe and non threatening environment, including issues related to 'Third World' countries and the economics of development. In addition to my college activities, I became an active member of our local United Nations Association.

Teaching a variety of enthusiastic learners was a great privilege and witnessing their growing confidence in their own ability, gave me enormous pleasure. This factor remained with me throughout my involvement in further and higher education. Sometime during that academic year, Jane informed me that she was expecting our second child. We were both looking forward to this and on 10th October 1972, Jane gave birth to our second daughter, Esme. As the two girls became a little older, we realised how different their respective temperaments were – Esme was much more independent in everything she did, compared to Amy, and this trait is still present today. At this juncture I should also mention that one of the pleasures of living in the north east of the country was its proximity to wonderful countryside and particularly the Yorkshire Dales. As a family, we were very fortunate that Jane's parents possessed a small cottage in Swale Dale in the village of 'Keld' where we spent many holidays with the children. I was subsequently very surprised that this was the environment of England I missed the most when we spent three years abroad. As the next academic year progressed, I became more involved with the United Nations Association both at the local level and regional level. My teaching of economic development issues and my involvement with the United Nations Association provided me with the opportunity to merge the two interests together by initiating and organising the first residential course, run by the college, for teachers/lecturers from all over the country. The one week residential course planned for June 1974 was scheduled to take place in Whitby, Yorkshire.

My focus on development economics was particularly directed towards Central and Southern Africa for obvious reasons. Thus began the urge, not only to participate and contribute to the development of a 'Third World' country but also go back to Southern Africa. South Africa was ruled out since the Apartheid laws would not have allowed me to live with my wife since she was 'White' and classified as 'European' and my children and I were classified as 'Non White' or 'Non European'. I had begun to explore other opportunities. The British Government's Department for Overseas Development and Administration were advertising and seeking lecturers to work in Southern Africa and elsewhere. I was fortunate that during this period, the Department advertised for a lecturer post to teach economics in Zambia which I applied for and was successful in being appointed. Before accepting the post, I applied for three years secondment from my post at Kirby College in Middlesbrough and this was agreed by both the College and the local authority. This ensured that when I returned from Zambia, I was guaranteed a post equivalent to the one I was leaving. Thus in the spring of 1974, Jane and I began preparations for this major change to our lives.

In the meantime, in addition to my normal teaching activities, I was busy preparing for the week's residential course in Whitby. In the first week of July 1974, when the programme commenced we were very fortunate that experts from a number of universities provided significant inputs, free of any costs, to the programme and this allowed all the participants not only to share their own good practice but also collectively develop new teaching material based on the specialist input. One interesting incident occurred mid way through the week when several participants came to me with an unusual request: they asked for the afternoon session to be postponed to the evening because they wished to watch a critical World Cup football match, taking place in West Germany, between Holland and Brazil for a place in the final. My response surprised them – I informed them that I was hoping someone would make that request since I also wanted to watch that particular match but could not interrupt the scheduled programme without their consent. The feedback from all the participants was excellent and particularly that it would enable them to refocus on their future teaching based on the expert input they received from the visiting lecturers. A few of them commented that watching the live semi-final football match was the 'icing on the cake'. My academic year ended on this high note.

Right to left: my late brother 'Doc', Amy, Me with 'stylish hair' and Esme before leaving UK

Shortly after that, Jane, Amy, Esme and I were busy with our final preparations for our new venture in Zambia. This included contacting estate agents for letting our property whilst we were away, purchasing clothes more suitable for a warmer climate and the commencement of malaria prevention tablets. Perhaps the most difficult part was visiting close family and friends and saying goodbye for the next three years.

CHAPTER 6

DEFENESTRATION

'Defenestration' is the act of throwing someone or something out of a window. The normal political use of the term implies the forcible or peremptory removal of an adversary or prisoner by throwing them out of a window.

When I began writing the story of my life and experiences, I thought that I would make a short passing reference about my friend and neighbour, Ahmed Timol who tragically lost his life in South Africa at the hands of the Security Police a week before his 30th birthday. However, once I embarked on the journey into what transpired and led to his premature death, I began to be aware of the enormous sense of anger which lay deeply buried in my subconscious by the concerns of everyday activity and living. Once I began writing, the hurtful truth began to surface like a sudden storm and even more questions began to emerge of the circumstances that led to his death. This then is the result. This narrative also reminded me, and I hope others, of the enormous sacrifice that hundreds of people made to give birth to a democratically elected South Africa despite the great hardship and pain they had to endure. Moreover, I am certain that had Ahmed lived, he would have been in a position to make a positive contribution to the new South Africa, but alas his life was cut short.

On Friday 29th October 1971, I arrived at College with no major concerns and proceeded to teach my Business Studies class during the first period of the day. After finishing my class, I went to our staff room and one of my colleagues had left his newspaper on his office desk with a glaring headline about a young Indian teacher 'Committing Suicide' by jumping out of the tenth story window of the infamous John Vorster Square police station in Johannesburg whilst in custody. When I read further to discover that the person who was alleged to have committed suicide was my friend and neighbour from Roodepoort, Ahmed Timol, I was in a state of immeasurable shock. I was in almost total shutdown but after a few minutes I gathered myself and immediately proceeded to the College library to read the full press report in private. Having read the article in full, I was in a confused and horrified emotional state – anger, disbelief, sadness, concern for his family, and grief all playing their respective role in my mind. After digesting the full horror of the story, I proceeded to the staff toilet, shut the door and quietly wept for the great loss of a friend and neighbour. At the lunch break, I walked to the post office, not far from the College, and sent a telegram to Ahmed Timol's family with a simple message of condolence and specifically 'None of us believe Ahmed committed suicide.' It is very unlikely that the telegram was delivered since the Apartheid Government police apparatus would most likely have intervened and confiscated this communication. I do not recall much of that fateful Friday after sending the telegram but managed to get through. I spent some time during that weekend endeavouring to find out from members of my family what actually transpired that led to this tragic loss of life. But in 1971 with the Apartheid Government's surveillance and oppression and the fact that during this period to make overseas phone calls meant you had to go through telephone operators on both sides, it was well nigh impossible to have an open and honest conversation over the telephone with anyone in my family in Roodepoort about what happened to Ahmed at that time.

I spent much of that weekend remembering my relationship with Ahmed Timol both as a friend and neighbour, whilst we were living in Roodepoort, South Africa as well the short period of time when Ahmed was in London. Ahmed Timol's family moved into flat No 2 of our family flats at 76 Mare Street, Roodepoort late in 1956. I lived in Flat No 1 with my parents and flats No 3 and No 5 were occupied by my two brothers, 'Joe' and Ebrahim and their respective families. Besides Ahmed and his parents, his three brothers and sister lived there as well. My most significant memory of Ahmed Timol was that he was an articulate, intelligent, compassionate and kind person who was very concerned about the iniquities of the Apartheid system. We discussed these issues in the evenings on the long stoep we shared on the flat and particularly the appalling consequences the Apartheid system inflicted upon 'Black' fellow South Africans. After I passed my driving test, Ahmed and I occasionally went out together socially. All the while we were friends and neighbours, we never disagreed about anything since we shared a similar outlook about the gross injustices perpetrated by the regime. He was also an accomplished cricketer and batsman whom I admired. Later he represented the Indian provincial side as well as playing for the 'Non White' South African team. Since he was one year ahead of me in school, I assumed that he was a year older than me, only to discover later that we were both born in November 1941 but he commenced schooling a year before I did. The relationship between the Choonara family members and the Timol family was always excellent and I personally enjoyed very good relations with the whole family and his mother, Hawa, was very kind and I recall that she frequently made fresh ginger beer for me, which I thoroughly enjoyed.

As I intimated earlier, my family and particularly my father placed a very heavy emphasis on encouraging all their children to continue their education and pursue a professional career. Unfortunately the year I successfully completed my Standard 8 year (equivalent to 'O' levels), the South African Apartheid Government prevented Indians from Roodepoort attending the Johannesburg Indian High School. There were very poor alternatives offered by the Apartheid Government, which I refused to consider enrolling for. This was even more galling in the light of the fact that the Indian community in South Africa were fully taxed and this tax was used to subsidise the 'White' population. This was a blow to my aspirations of completing my matriculation and progressing on to higher education. There was a High School in Roodepoort but it was for 'Whites' only. Ahmed Timol was fortunately in the last cohort to be accepted at the Johannesburg Indian High School and after two years of study, he successfully completed his matriculation examinations in December 1959. He postponed his desire to go into higher education for a year in order to supplement his family income. About that time, Ahmed and my friend and cricket captain Yusuf 'Jo Jo' Saloojee (who in a democratic and free South Africa became an Ambassador for the Government) encouraged me to join the Roodepoort Study Circle. The Study Circle was made up of a small group of people spearheaded by two local young activists whom I knew and its principal aim was raising our political awareness through discussing contemporary and historical political issues as well as inviting guest speakers. Most of the Study Circle activities were conducted without publicity since the 'elders' in the Roodepoort Indian community would not have allowed these activities on its premises for fear of Apartheid's security apparatus. The meetings normally ended with the group singing the national anthem of the African National Congress -"Nkosi sikele 'Afrika" which later appropriately became the national anthem of South Africa.

In 1961 having obtained a scholarship, Ahmed commenced his teaching course at the Johannesburg Training Institute for Indian Teachers. Ahmed was very active in most of the political and social activities of the Teacher Training Institute and was elected Vice Chairman of the Students Representative Council. This frequently brought him into conflict with the establishment. In early January 1962 I said farewell to my family and friends and left South Africa. Little did I realise then that I would next meet up with Ahmed Timol both in London and Cambridge in the late 1960's. After leaving South Africa, the two people in

South Africa I corresponded with were Ahmed Timol and my last girl friend, 'Hassina' who incidentally was introduced to me by Ahmed. My correspondence with Ahmed, besides enquiring about family welfare, was predominantly focussed on political philosophy and particularly socialism. It was very apparent to me that Ahmed was passionately concerned, as I was, about the great injustices suffered by black Africans in their own country and the international capitalist system which supported and sustained it. I found his letters very informative and this encouraged me to continue my Anti-Apartheid activities in England. My correspondence with Hassina was short lived since we both realized that I was very unlikely to return to South Africa. Ahmed completed his teacher training course in 1963 and commenced his teaching career at Roodepoort Indian School. He

Ahmed receiving his certificate and the message which I value highly

was obviously pleased to have achieved his teaching qualification and the photograph of his graduation he sent me clearly indicates that.

Shortly after Ahmed commenced teaching, 'Jo Jo' Saloojee joined the school as a teacher and the two of them established a very close working relationship as well as making their older students more politically aware of the great injustices suffered by their fellow South Africans. I am almost certain that the senior staff of the school would not approve of this for fear of the security police.

During the period 1963 to 1966, political life for people fighting for a liberated South Africa became increasingly difficult with the Security Branch intervening and interrogating activists for the flimsiest reasons. After Ahmed's friend 'Jo Jo' left for Zambia, he also made the decision to leave the country. In April 1967 he arrived in England and later that year he and I met in London. He briefed me regarding the increasingly oppressive actions of the Apartheid Government in South Africa as well as bringing me news of family and friends. On one of the occasions I met him in London, I recall that we went to meet a friend of mine from Manchester called 'Rita' who was training to be a nurse. He explained that he was living with fellow South Africans in a house in Kensington and that he was teaching in a school for recent immigrants in Slough. As I was completing my final year at university, whilst we kept in touch, I did not see him again until July 1968. I was pleased and honoured that Ahmed Timol came to my wedding held in Cambridge on 15 July 1968. I still treasure several

Below, Ahmed second from right, Jane and Dave Collins.

photographs of the wedding which mark Ahmed's presence – on the right opposite.

Little did I realise then, that this would be the last time I would see him alive! During the period September 1968 to July 1969, I commenced and completed my Post Graduate Certificate in Education to enable me to begin a teaching career in further education.

It was much later that I learnt that in February 1969, Ahmed left for Moscow to attend the International Lenin School to learn about the various important aspects of the liberation struggle. It is worth noting that 'Black', 'Brown', and 'White' South Africans were attracted to the Communist Party in the 1960's and the two decades after that, not only for ideological reasons but also because the Soviet Union was one of a few Governments in the whole of the Northern Hemisphere willing to provide practical support to the many southern African nations in their fight for liberation. Whilst in the West, although there was strong support for the liberation struggle from liberal minded people, most of these states and their respective overseas corporations were more preoccupied with the ideology of "Profit at almost any cost" than the welfare of the vast majority of people who lived under this yoke. It was during this period in Moscow that Ahmed met and was a contemporary of Thabo Mbeki, who succeeded Nelson Mandela, as President of South Africa. Having completed his studies at the Lenin School in Moscow in October 1969, Ahmed returned to London for a short period.

He surprised his family and everyone on the flat by returning to Roodepoort, South Africa, without prior warning, in February 1970. I suspect that in the 1960's and 1970's in the context of the 'Cold War', that persons going from London to Moscow and returning nine months later, regardless of the circuitous routes they follow, would be on the radar of the security services in the UK. I equally suspect there existed a degree of cooperation between the security services of the UK and the South African security services and that Ahmed Timol's visit to Moscow would have been noted by the former and communicated to the latter. If this was the case, then Ahmed would be under surveillance from day one when he returned to South Africa. My suspicion of this is partly reinforced by the fact that when I applied for British Citizenship in 1968, two 'plain clothes officers' interviewed me at my flat in Hull and one particular concern they enquired about was 'why did you make visits to Communist Poland during 1966 and 1967?' Since I cannot remember documenting my visit anywhere, I was unable to work out where they gathered this information from. In any case, they appeared to be satisfied when I informed them that I was visiting a friend in Wroclaw in Poland and also that my sister-in-law in London was originally from Poland. In other words, whilst Ahmed may have lain low initially, he would almost certainly be watched by the Special Branch even after he returned to teaching at the Roodepoort Indian High School in April 1970. I gathered from friends that Ahmed gradually increased his political activities, predominantly producing and distributing leaflets to students and other activists. He strongly advocated that all people were born equal and should have equal political rights and people needed to take active steps to promote and further this aim. Furthermore, the message he conveyed was that there was no scientific basis to sustain the myth of the superiority of 'White People' over other ethnic groups. These kind of logical and sensible messages were obviously an anathema to the Apartheid Government and therefore needed to be stopped since it undermined the very foundations of apartheid. Ahmed was helped in this activity by Salim Essop, a medical student, who lived close by.

On the evening of Friday 22nd October 1971, Ahmed and his friend Salim Essop on their way home from Johannesburg by car, were stopped at a police roadblock and their car was searched for political literature. It was very likely that Ahmed was under surveillance and the police roadblock was planned. They were arrested and taken to Newlands Police Station. There appears to be contradictory evidence of whether there was any political literature left in the car – a creditable suggestion was that it was 'planted by the authorities' from Ahmed's intercepted communication to provide them with an excuse for the arrest. They were charged at the Police Station with distributing banned ANC (African National Congress) literature, copies of secret communication correspondence, instruction received from the Communist Party in London and so on... Ahmed was a member of both these political organisations. It is likely that Security Branch officers were either already there or arrived shortly after. Ahmed and Salim were separated. and going on past experiences and knowledge of White police behaviour and brutality, I would not be surprised to learn that they were severely assaulted even before questioning began in order to intimidate and 'soften them up'. After several hours, both of them and the material alleged to have been found in their car was taken to the purpose built, infamous, ten stories John Vorster Square Security Police Headquarters. They were in effect being detained indefinitely without a trial and in solitary confinement. According to the draconian South African laws, no court, lawyers or family had the right of access to the detainees. This was then, I assume, the beginning of their worst nightmares and not only were they now subjected to additional physical assaults but systematic torture that would eventually lead to Ahmed Timol's unnecessary and untimely death as well as long term trauma for his family and friends.

Shortly after arriving at the John Vorster Square Security Police Headquarters, their interrogation commenced and some of them involved have been cited numerous times at detainee inquests. Whilst interrogation of suspects is a normal practice of security officers in most countries of the world, however, when this interrogation is accompanied by intensive and extensive violence then it demeans the society that allows this to happen. Both Ahmed and Salim were tortured over several days and the methods, I assume, included the notorious 'standing torture' when detainees are prevented from sitting down or sleeping, electric shock to various parts of the body including the genital areas, cigarette burns to various parts of the body, hanging out detainees out of upper floor windows by their ankles and threatening to throw them down, covering detainees heads with bags and then subjecting them to other forms of torture, extracting of finger nails and perhaps other forms of torture unknown to normal and ordinary civilians. It is interesting to note that during the 1950's and even the early 1960's, whilst police brutality was common, the systematic torture by the security agencies emerged in the 1960's and was 'refined' in the early 1970's.

According to my late brother 'Joe' Security Police knocked on his front door on Saturday 23 October and asked for Mr. and Mrs. Timol and were informed that they live in Flat 2. They began heatedly questioning them about Ahmed then proceeded to search his room and confiscated several personal items including his passport, typewriter and personal documents. My brother Ebrahim, returning from morning prayer, noticed that something was amiss in the Timol household. The Timol family were informed that Ahmed was in detention and Ahmed's father and younger brother were then taken to Foster Square for questioning. They returned after several hours. During the next few days a total of 115 people from all walks of life and all nationalities, who were all opposed to the Apartheid Government's perception and draconian policies were arrested in various parts of the country including Ahmed's brother Mohammed who had left a few days earlier for Durban – some of those arrested in Roodepoort were contemporaries of mine. Mohammed Timol was interrogated at length over the next two days using various methods of torture as well as being physically assaulted. In addition to the wide scale arrests, interrogation, assault and torture there were also searches for 'underground' literature at most of the institutions where many of the detainees either attended or worked. This paranoiac over-reaction by the Security Police in South Africa, a common feature of despotic regimes, was perhaps designed to frighten others from protesting.

There were further searches of the Timol flat on Saturday and during the next two days, the searches continued including searching all the dustbins of the flat, the roof of the flats and my family were asked to open their storeroom under the stairs. The domestic help from all the flats were then coerced to sign a statement that Ahmed asked them to distribute leaflets in the then African Township. Later on the same day, the 27 October 1971, the Security Police came back to the flat and informed Ahmed's mother, Hawa, that Ahmed was dead. They proceeded to tell her the absurd story that his death was a result of **Ahmed attempting to escape by jumping out of 10th floor window at the John Vorster Square security police building.** Ahmed's mother was also told that she needed to inform her husband that Ahmed's body was at the Government Mortuary in Johannesburg. Even now I cannot begin to imagine the anguish, torment, pain, distress, anger and, bewilderment experienced by his parents and family. My brothers and their respective families living on the flat were all greatly alarmed by the turn of events and felt the pain for the sudden tragedy suffered by their neighbour and friend. For some of them, particularly my brother Ebrahim, this turned into hateful anger of the Security Police and all those that supported this cruel regime.

There is a profound difference between the Apartheid state's version and the reality which led to Ahmed's premature death. There is a very strong possibility that after several days of extreme torture, Ahmed may have been barely alive. If this is correct then a more plausible explanation of what occurred on the tenth floor of the John Voster Square building, is that he was unconscious or even dead and they dragged him to a room with an external window to carry out their evil deeds. Ahmed's friend Essop Salim was severely tortured and he was taken on a stretcher from the John Voster Square building to the Johannesburg General Hospital where medical staff noted that he was severely assaulted. Essop Salim was charged under the Terrorism Act over a year later and sentenced to five years which he served on Robben Island. If this was the treatment meted out to Essop Salim, then going on the notorious reputation of the John Voster Square security officers for torture and brutality, it is extremely likely that Ahmed Timol, their main detainee, was subjected to the most inhumane treatment imaginable. My personal interpretation of his death is that he was interrogated and tortured over several days and nights and they attempted to extract the maximum information about the underground activities of both the South African Communist Party and the ANC they thought Ahmed was engaged in. Sometime during this intensive and continuous torture they killed him either accidently or with intentions to teach 'these bloody Coolies (an insulting term used to denote Indians) a lesson'. In these circumstances it would be reasonable to suggest that in their panic they concocted the absurd story that he committed suicide by jumping out of the tenth story window.

The fact that the police immediately surrounded the area where the body fell points to the very high probability they were waiting in the lobby of the building, on instructions, so no other person/s could see the state of the body or intervene in their outrageous and diabolical plans and deeds. According to my family, the injuries to Ahmed's body were inconsistent with the injuries that would be sustained by someone jumping out of window – injuries such as bruises and burn marks all over his body, his hand nails removed and above all, his eye out of its socket. Independent and eminent pathologist and medical experts all concluded that the extensive injuries to Ahmed's body could not be explained by the fall out of the window. The absurdity of the Apartheid Government's treachery can be best conveyed by the ridiculous summary of the inquest magistrate, when he stated that there was no foul play by the police and "Although he was questioned for hours, he was treated in a civilised and humane manner." I frequently wonder how lackeys like him can sleep at night.

A forensic analysis of the available evidence leads to only one conclusion: that Ahmed Timol was murdered by the Security Police based in the Forster Square building in Johannesburg. Whilst Ahmed was the first detainee to die a violent death at John Vorster Square, five other detainees subsequently also lost their lives while being detained and interrogated there. No one has ever been charged or brought to trial for any of these deaths/murders. Many other activists, in a variety of locations in South Africa, also died whilst in custody and the Apartheid Government's invariable response was that they committed suicide. On the 'South African History Online' site there is an extensive list of names of people who died in detention. Besides this appalling fact, there were one hundred and thirty one 'official' executions of opponents of apartheid in this period.

After Ahmed's death there were rumours that the South African Security Police refined their torture methods with the aid of foreign security services and particularly the Israeli security services. These rumours, to my knowledge, have never been substantiated but they arose because there was significant collaboration between the two governments regarding developing and utilising defence equipment. Regardless of this, I find it incomprehensible that the Israeli government would wish to collaborate with and/or assist the Apartheid Government at any level for a number of reasons. Firstly, many Jewish South Africans fought against the apartheid system. The examples that immediately spring to mind include, Albie Sachs, who lost his right arm and an eye when his car was blown up by security agents of the Apartheid Government, Ruth First, who was killed by a letter bomb sent to her place of work by the orders of a South African policeman, Joe Slovo, Denis Goldberg and Helen Joseph who fought tirelessly for a democratically elected government illustrate the degree of commitment and sacrifice Jewish South Africans made in the fight against apartheid. Many of them also suffered lengthy periods in detention. Secondly, it was common knowledge that many of the leaders of the Nationalist Party which formed the Government after 1948 elections were ardent supporters of Nazi Germany during the Second World War. The same Nazis who were responsible for the cruel deaths of millions of Jewish people shared with the Apartheid regime a similar ideology of the 'superior race'. The Conservative Prime Minister, Harold Macmillan recognised that 'The Wind of Change' was blowing across Africa in a speech he made to the South African Parliament in Cape Town on 3 February 1960, hence I find it incomprehensible that the policy of successive Conservative administrations provided tacit support for the South African Apartheid Government for decades. This support was best illustrated by Prime Minister Thatcher's labelling of the ANC under Nelson Mandela, as a 'terrorist organisation.' Furthermore, this implicit support undervalued the sacrifices made by thousands upon thousands of British citizens during the Second World War in their fight against Hitler and his pursuit of the evil ideology of the 'superior race'.

Ahmed was buried in Roodepoort Cemetery on Friday 29 October 1971. According to my family, his funeral was one of the biggest funerals ever held in Roodepoort with all Indian businesses closed as a mark of respect. People from all over the country attended his funeral but there was also a heavy police presence. The most heart-rending element for the Timol family on that day was not only the burial of their eldest son but also that Ahmed's beloved brother Mohammed was not even temporarily allowed out of detention to attend the funeral – he was eventually released on 14 March 1972 without any charge. In the mid 1970's, during my secondment to Zambia for three years, I paid a short visit to South Africa to visit my mother and family. During this visit, I visited Ahmed's mother, Hawa, with my brother Ebrahim in order to express my condolences in person. I think that Haroon, Ahmed's younger brother was present on the day of my visit. The sad and abiding memory of my short visit was that a kind, considerate and vibrant person was now so different from her previous self – she had not only aged more than her years but also Ahmed's death had taken an enormous toll on her health and well-being. Her appearance at the Truth and Reconciliation Commission, which can be viewed on U-Tube, where she makes a heart rendering plea for someone to provide her with answers for the reason why her son died, is followed with nothing but complete silence. The perpetrators responsible for Ahmed's death made no attempts to attend the Commission to tell the truth. Whilst the Truth and Reconciliation Commission in South Africa played an important role in healing many wrongs of the past, in the case of Ahmed Timol's death, too many questions remain unanswered. My personal feeling on this is 'without truth, there is no justice, no reconciliation, no healing and no closure'.

I was pleased to learn that Ahmed's contribution and struggle for an apartheid free and democratically elected government was acknowledged over recent years in different ways. The late President Nelson Mandela opened and renamed a high school in Azaadville as the 'Ahmed Timol Secondary School' in 1999. President Thabo Mbeki was very clear about

Ahmed's contribution in his 'Introduction' to the outstanding book written by Imtiaz Cajee entitled 'Timol – A Quest for Justice'. In 2009, Ahmed was posthumously awarded The National Order of Luthuli for his excellent contribution and selfless sacrifice during the struggle against apartheid.

On reflection, whilst Ahmed Timol and I were both born in November 1941, lived as neighbours and friends for many years, the events and outcomes of our lives exemplifies my earlier statement that 'The Cycle of Life 'is made up of three critical constituents – circumstances, choices, and consequences. On the one hand, in my case, because of circumstances, I made a choice of pursuing a career in further education in England which led to outcomes which have been fairly good. On the other hand, Ahmed made a more noble choice which unfortunately led to appalling consequences.

Whilst this narrative is a small digression from the story of my own life, my friend's untimely and cruel death had a profound and long term effect on his family, his friends and me and my South African family and that is my primary reason I have included it here. The additional reason is to acknowledge the great sacrifice people like Ahmed had made to challenge the evils of state oppression and the ideology supporting this in my country of birth. In addition to personal knowledge gathered from my long interaction with Ahmed, additional information was secured from a variety of sources for this chapter. My immediate family and friends in Roodepoort were generous with sharing their knowledge of this dreadful event with me. The excellent book written by Ahmed's nephew, Imtiaz Cajee entitled 'Timol – A Quest for Justice' is an important source for readers who wish to fully comprehend the background and circumstances that led to Ahmed's death. The very informative website, 'South African History Online', Wikipedia, a recently released DVD entitled 'Indians Can't Fly' and the U Tube coverage of 'The Truth and Reconciliation Commission's work, all provided valuable information regarding Ahmed's untimely death. Mohammed Timol, his brother Ismail and Imtiaz Ahmed Cajee kindly read this chapter and suggested some amendments. I am grateful to all these sources and needless to say that the errors, omissions, interpretation and opinions expressed are my sole responsibility.

Postscript

I understand, from the news emanating from South Africa, that 46 years after Ahmed's death, an inquest into his death has been reopened in July 2017 because of new evidence. In addition to the evidence given by a variety of witnesses which undermined the notion that Ahmed committed suicide, the post mortem conducted on him and the evidence of the injuries, the inquest heard, were not consistent with the ones caused by his fall from the 10th floor of John Voster Square. The forensic pathologist, Dr Holland testified that the injuries must have been present prior to the fall. Dr Holland performed between 4000 to 5000 post mortems during her career and she confirmed that the multiple injuries present on Ahmed's body were sustained during a physical assault while in police custody before his death. She stated that some of the wounds appeared to be older than 12 hours, while others were sustained four to five days before the fatal fall. She also revealed that Ahmed had an injury to the skull, which might have been caused by a blunt object.

On 12th October 2017, Judge Billy Mothle announced that based on the evidence presented at the inquest, Ahmed Timol was murdered by the secuirty officers based at John Voster Square. Now, after 46 years, the truth, which all those who knew Ahmed will never have doubted, brings to an end the years of denial.

CHAPTER SEVEN

A TO Z 'AHMED TO ZAMBIA'

The Zambian Airways flight to Lusaka in August 1974 was a long and an uneventful flight. As we were flying over the country, both Jane I were surprised and commented that much of the landscape appeared as burnt brown and yellow in colour and this was in stark contrast to the green colours of the English landscape we had just left. I had obviously forgotten that this was the normal colour of the 'Veld 'in South Africa during the dry season. We were met at the airport by Ian, who was the Head of the Business Studies Department of Evelyn Hone College, Lusaka. He drove us to the College Hotel and explained to us that we would be staying there for a short period of time. The medium size and comfortable hotel was across the road from the college and was used by the college for hotel and hospitality training purposes. This was our 'home' for a few weeks. Shortly after that we were provided with a three bedroom semi-detached bungalow on a site called 'Kwacha Flats', one of six bungalows which shared the site, in the suburb of Kabulonga located a few miles from Lusaka. An important feature of the site was that three of the bungalows were occupied by Zambians and the other three by overseas families. This predominantly residential area was where we lived happily for the next three years.

My teaching duties did not commence immediately and as a new recruit there were inevitable administrative things to complete with the College, the Department of Vocational Education in Lusaka and the bank. I was also advised to purchase a car as soon as possible since the public transport system was in its infancy and not very reliable. This short period before my teaching commenced, allowed us to explore parts of Lusaka. This was the largest city in Zambia as well as being the Capital and commercial centre of the country. In late August, we were aware that the weather was beginning to warm up, but Lusaka being over 4000 feet above sea level, the climate was fairly pleasant at that time of the year. It is October onwards when the humidity rises, just before the wet season that even local people begin to complain of the heat and humidity. During the 'wet season' with very high humidity, the college began earlier in the morning – 7.30 a.m. starting time was not unusual – and finished early afternoon. The arrival of rain was welcomed by all

Evelyn Hone College was a relatively modern college based on a campus with good teaching accommodation for students and staff as well some residential accommodation, on site, for students and staff. I soon learnt that at the time of Independence (October 1964), Zambia was poorly served with qualified and skilled personnel and that there were less than a hundred graduates in the country. In this environment, education became a priority in nation building. The college was staffed by people from a significant number of different countries – African, Asian and European. This multi-national and multi-cultural environment of the college meant that we were given the opportunity to enjoy each other's company as well as learning from each other. The student body was predominantly made up of Zambians but there was a significant number of students in the Business Studies Department from Zimbabwe (Ian Smith's Southern Rhodesia then) and the age range was eighteen plus. The college focus was on teaching further and higher education courses predominantly to full time students with a small element of part-time courses. Since my arrival at the college was when three quarters of the academic year was already completed, I was eased into the teaching role at that point. My main role was teaching Economics to Accountancy and Business Studies students.

Once the new academic year commenced and I was fully immersed in the work of the department, my interaction with the students was both exciting and rewarding and I was personally inspired by their enthusiasm and commitment to learning. The value they placed on education was extraordinary. Many of the local students who were not residents on the campus would walk many miles to the college and walk back home again in the late evening. They would study in the library long after their respective courses ended for the day because they had no electricity or lights at home. As the academic year progressed and when I returned marked assignments, many of the students requested another similar one for me to mark, so that they could further hone-in their assignment writing skills in preparation for their final examination. Whilst this increased my workload, I was inspired by them and their commitment to improve their performance. The students were obviously eager to do well in their accountancy qualifications since they were acutely aware of the high correlation between a good qualification and securing a well paid post in either the private sector or the growing public sector.

During this period I was also informed that the college was involved in a World Bank sponsored educational renewal project specifically related to the Diploma in Accountancy course. Since I was teaching Economics on this course, I enquired about the status of this subject and the progress in writing the new curriculum for it. I was informed by the Head of Department that George (who was also a British sponsored lecturer on either his second or third spell in Zambia) who also taught economics in the department and Alan a private sector bookkeeper/accountant were progressing with this task. Out of professional curiosity I asked them for a copy of their proposed economics curriculum for the Diploma in Accountancy. On reading their first draft of the proposed economics curriculum for the accountancy course, I was shocked by the contents – the contents appeared to be simply grafted out of a fairly dated Economics textbook. I was further stunned by the inclusion of 'The Ship Building Industry' in the proposed economics curriculum, given that Zambia is a landlocked country. I was also bewildered by their failure to include any local economic activity and particularly the Copper Industry and its vital role in the Zambian economy as over 90% of its foreign earnings were derived from this.

After spending some time agonising about what I could do to address this wholly inadequate proposal, I wrote a letter to the Head of Vocational Education in the Department of Education, outlining my concerns. I was invited to a meeting with the Head and his team and we discussed my concerns in some detail. They agreed that the proposals were grossly inadequate for this World Bank sponsored project but were at a loss about how to address the problem since they did not know anyone in the sector who could do this work. At that juncture, the Head of Vocational Education asked me 'would you be willing to undertake this task?' I requested some time to think about it. The following day after careful consideration, I agreed to start afresh and write the Economics component of The Diploma in Accountancy programme. Whilst this was unpaid work on top of my normal teaching duties, I found this extremely rewarding and stimulating. After several months of research and writing, I completed this work. I was pleased when my proposed curriculum was accepted and to the best of my knowledge, used for several years after my departure from Zambia.

Whilst the majority of people working on British aid projects in Zambia, and possibly elsewhere, were well qualified and up to date on the professional competencies, there were others whose motivation and contribution to developing countries was questionable. I became acutely aware of this issue in conversation with some British sponsored aid personnel working for the Government Printers in

Lusaka. The government Printing Press was located very near Evelyn Hone College and the British printers stationed there frequently had their lunch and coffee breaks in the College's staff common room. In discussions with them, one of them commented on the work they were engaged in and clearly stated that they enjoyed working there, receiving a reasonably good local salary and a fairly large sum, tax free, from the U.K. Government. More significant was his statement that whilst one of the main objectives of their work was to train Zambians to take over from them, they were in 'no hurry' to do this since they could not secure such lucrative contracts elsewhere. I must reiterate that they appeared to be exceptional and that the vast majority of sponsored aid personnel were dedicated to enabling local people to develop their skills and knowledge in order that they could take over responsibility for their respective organisations.

In the period 1970 to 1990, Zambia and Tanzania were at the forefront of providing training bases for the South African liberation struggle and the outskirts of Lusaka was an important base. Whilst I was aware of this, I made the decision not to be involved in this struggle for two reasons: firstly, my experience coupled to my commitment was about education as an agent for empowering local people; secondly, I was also acutely aware that there were people I came into contact with who may have been either agents of the South African Apartheid Government or sympathisers. In this context, I recall an interesting episode which reinforced my stance. At an Economics Seminar held at one of the large hotels in Lusaka, with a Government Minister present, at the Question and Answer Session, I made several comments about the need for supporting economic research based on empirical evidence which is openly available for validation. After the seminar, an officer from the American Embassy introduced himself and we exchanged contact details. Shortly after that, Jane and I were invited to dinner at this person's residence. There were several couples at this event and after the meal, our host suggested that all the men retire upstairs for 'drink and chit chat'. I was then introduced to the people present who included someone from 'Security' and someone from the British Embassy. An interesting aspect of this encounter was that several of the people present began to question me about my position regarding the liberation struggle in South Africa. I made my views about the evils of 'Apartheid' clear and reinforced this with the fact that Jane and I could not visit my family together in South Africa and that the reason I went to England to study was that I was not able to do this in South Africa. My observation and conclusion from this encounter was that 'they' may have come to the conclusion that I was unlikely to be 'useful' to them regarding passing on to them information regarding the liberation struggle in South Africa. A few days after this episode, however, I received a request from the American officer to supply him with a list of all members of staff at Evelyn Hone College. My reply was short and swift informing him that he needed to address his request to the Principal of Evelyn Hone College and not me. After that, I no longer heard from him. Equally interesting at the time was that many Ugandan African intelligentsia relocated themselves in Zambia, and Lusaka in particular, as refugees fleeing from Idi Amin. A significant number of them worked in the education and health sectors and their contribution was fully appreciated by the local people.

Very shortly after we arrived in Zambia, I was introduced by Ian to the 'Lusaka Club' which he informed me was worth joining since most of the British expatriates, living in Lusaka, belonged to it and it was a centre for social activities. After discussing this with Jane, we both agreed that we would not join since this defeated our wish to learn more about local life and the challenges they faced. This social 'cocoon life' was further reinforced by a party we threw. Sometime after settling in to our home in Kwacha Flats, we threw a party for our friends. The most interesting aspect of this event was when a Zambian friend stated to me that, 'I have never been to any party in Zambia where there were so many White people' and equally interesting was a comment by an English friend who stated that I have lived in Zambia for a number of years now and I have never been to a party with so many Zambians present'. This brought home to me the realisation that this is a feature with most ex-patriot communities where they tend to stick together socially, and where possible, geographically.

Early in my second year in Zambia, I made a short trip to Roodepoort, South Africa flying with Botswana Airways to Johannesburg. Jane, Amy, and Esme remained in Lusaka since under Apartheid laws they would not be allowed to stay with my family. This brief visit not only allowed me to see my mother, brothers and their respective families but also friends. One particular visit was especially important for me

– a visit to my late friend's mother, Mrs Timol. The murder of her son and my friend Ahmed Timol had a dreadful impact on her life. An interesting event that occurred during this short visit was when I was asked by my friend Mohammed Valliallah's father whether his son, who was completing his training to be a doctor in Cairo, could possibly do his 'housemanship' in Zambia since the South African Government did not recognised the Egyptian qualification. I informed him that if this was possible, then I would get in touch with him and Mohammed could come and live with us in Lusaka. On my return, after making the appropriate enquiries it was confirmed that this was not only possible but welcomed since Zambia was very short of doctors at that time. I discussed this with Jane and we agreed that Mohammed could live with us for a period of time until he found his own accommodation.

Mohammed's arrival in Lusaka did not put a lot of pressure on our accommodation since the bungalow had three bedrooms. Very shortly after his arrival and all the necessary paperwork was completed, he began to work at Lusaka General Hospital. On returning home after his first night on duty in the A & E department, he informed us of his experience. He stated that his first three patients all involved episodes of biting: His first patient was an older European lady, possibly Greek, who did not speak much English and she shifted her arm to near her mouth and with a biting motion made a sound 'meow meow' , Mohammed determined that she was bitten by a cat and treated her with the appropriate medicine. The second patient suffered from a more common bite in

Zambia: a snake bite, and after questioning the patient about the kind of snake involved, he proceeded to give him the appropriate treatment and discharged him from the hospital. His third patient in succession suffered, what Mohammed termed the most severe biting case of the night, was of a young man with part of his ear lobe hanging loose. Mohammed enquired of the man, what had caused this? The man sheepishly informed him that he and his wife were having a passionate love making affair and his wife got carried away and bit his ear lobe. Needless to say his wife was not present at the hospital and Mohammed stitched the ear lobe on and discharged him with some words of caution he needed to employ in the future when making love to his young wife.

The coincidences of three successive bite cases on his first night on duty in A & E was fortunately never repeated again. Mohammed also informed us of severe shortages in the hospital including the effect that was having on patient care. He gave us an insight into the difficult decisions that Doctors have to make in those circumstances – for example, he stated that because of the shortage of 'incubators' they had to accommodate several premature babies in one incubator with the added potential complications of cross infection. During this period, Mohammed also introduced us to Mr. and Mrs. Arthur. Mr. Arthur was an eminent Australian neuro-surgeon who was based in Lusaka. To the best of my recollection, he may have been the only neuro-surgeon in Zambia in the mid 1970's. He was dedicated to his work but found it increasingly frustrating when the shortage of essential items such as anaesthetics were unavailable for him to perform his surgery. At times the shortages of goods also related to simple domestic items such as cooking oil, etc. In these circumstances, when any of us went shopping and supplies were delivered, we shopped for our friends as well for ourselves. I distinctly remember that on one of these occasions, Mr. Arthur, Zambia's only neuro-surgeon, burst into our house exclaiming he had bought us twelve toilet rolls as they had been delivered that day to the supermarket. We learnt early on in our stay in Zambia, that the supply and shortage of many imported products depended on the fluctuation in copper prices in European and Far Eastern capitals, since over 90% of Zambia's foreign earnings were from this source.

Sometime at the end of my first year I was informed by my brother that my mother was visiting family in Lilongwe, in Malawi and would like to visit us as well. Jane and I decided that during the short holiday break we could drive down to Malawi and return with my mother to Lusaka. I was informed by a family friend in Lusaka that we may wish to stop in the border town of Chipata and have a meal with an 'Indian' family there who knew my family in South Africa. When we arrived at the house, we were very warmly welcomed and the 'uncle' said that he remembered me as a little boy when he visited us in South Africa and he was very grateful to my father since he introduced him to his future wife and he had a very happy marriage. The short stop was very fortunate since I forgot to bring my 'Blue Book' to enable the car to cross the border. I informed our host and considered asking the Choonara family in Malawi to pick us up at the border but our host said this was not necessary. He then produced the key to his relatively new large car and insisted that we take his car with the necessary papers and spend a few days in Malawi relaxing. I was stunned by the generosity of my host and after a very enjoyable meal, we set off on the narrow and part dirt track road to Lilongwe in Malawi.

On driving back at the border crossing, the immigration officer stated that my mother would have to have a variety of inoculations to enter Zambia. We enquired about this and the officer brought out a glass bowl with the necessary needles, etc. but obviously these had not been used for a considerable time and were extremely dirty. I asked the officer how much would it cost to inoculate my mother and he stated 25 Kwacha. We made the decision that the treatment was more likely to make my mother ill then prevent her from being ill. Having considered the risk, I queried the cost of not proceeding with the inoculation and was informed by the officer that this would cost 50 Kwacha. We chose the latter option. Thankfully, he agreed and after that my 70 year old mother's trip to Lusaka was uneventful. After about three weeks staying with us, she was scheduled to fly back to Malawi. Since I was unable to take her because of work commitments, Jane drove my mother to Lusaka Airport and ensured that she was safely on board for her flight before returning home. In the middle of the night we were woken up with a loud knock on the door and a friend from College explain to us that my mother was in the car. She was extremely tired having flown over a sizable part of Zambia when the plane developed engine problems in the Copperbelt and returned to Lusaka. Since she could not direct people to where we lived, she explained to the other Asian passenger on board where I worked and eventually located this colleague who brought her home. In one day my mother saw more of Zambia than we had managed and Jane took her back to the airport the next day for her rescheduled flight. In years two and three, Jane was involved in a variety of voluntary projects and particularly in education. It was because of this interest that she spearheaded and ran a nursery school in a stationary bus located in the suburbs of Lusaka. This experience may also have been a factor contributing to her return to Zambia later in life.

In many ways living and working in Zambia provided Jane, Amy, Esme and me with opportunities to explore this vast and beautiful country during the vacations. We made several trips to 'Mosie O Tania' more commonly known as Victoria Falls and Livingstone. Amy and Esme were very young and were fascinated not only by the majesty of the waterfalls but also by the freely roaming and over friendly monkeys. I vividly recall that, whilst sitting in the back of our little Fiat car and whilst Jane and I were out of the car, they began to offer the monkeys bananas. The cheeky monkeys were not satisfied being offered one or two bananas from the bunch in the car, they simply dived through the open window and began helping themselves. Jane and I heard the children's screams, rushed to the car and got the children out of the car and eventually the uninvited guest. On another break we decided to visit the South Luangwa Game Reserve – a very large game reserve several hundred miles from Lusaka. We did not book any accommodation and looking at the map, we decided that we would enquire at a place called 'The Chinchilla Lodge' which was located on a substantial hill overlooking the river. On arrival at the lodge, we were greeted by the lodge manager. He first enquired whether we had booked but before I could reply he gave me a very large smile and stated that he recognised me from the time when we lived in Evelyn Hone College Hotel where he completed his training. This was most fortuitous and he stated that he would ensure that our stay at the lodge was enjoyable. He informed us that he could not give us the President's apartment but he would give us the Prime Minister's apartment. We were surprised and very pleased at the turn of events and our visit was enjoyable and memorable.

One other vacation break was equally memorable for different reasons. We booked a week's holiday on the shores of Lake Tanzanika – a vast natural lake bordering Zambia and Tanzania. After booking in and having an early evening meal, we were escorted to our 'Rondaval' , a small round building with a thatched roof. We were making ourselves comfortable and preparing to go to bed when the walls of the Rondaval began to shake on one side. We were surprised, shocked and bewildered by this and as we looked out of the window, all we could see was large grey mass covering the whole of the large window. After a while, the vibration gradually faded away. Early next morning we enquired at the reception desk and they assured us that this was nothing to be worried about. It was just the elephants rubbing their itches away on the Rondaval walls as they passed through the village. We were not very assured by this and we decided not to venture out at night to find out. The other interesting aspect of this holiday was that when we wished to swim in the lake, we were always escorted by an armed guard since the lake was also a home to hippos and crocodiles. In brief, Jane and I agreed that whilst we were living in Zambia, we must explore this beautiful country as extensively as we could afford to.

In my second and third years, in addition to developing a new Economics curriculum for the Diploma in Accountancy, I was also asked to be an external examiner for this subject as well as having a full teaching timetable. The work was stimulating and rewarding particularly when I witnessed the progress of these dedicated students. As my three years contract was nearing completion, I was asked by a number of people in the Department of Vocational Education to extend my stay in Zambia. I was then faced with a dilemma. I enjoyed working in Zambia but my secondment was limited to three years and coupled to that, Jane and I felt that as Amy and Esme were rapidly growing up they would benefit from going to school in England. It was also during this period that Jane informed me that she was pregnant. It was in this context that we decided that we had to return to England. We agreed that we would fly back to England early in June since we were expecting the birth of our third child in July. In brief, with a mixture of excitement, trepidation and sadness we returned to England in early June 1977.

CHAPTER EIGHT

THE RETURN

The abiding memory of returning to our home in Linthorpe, Middlesbrough was the warm welcome we received from our neighbours on Bentick Avenue. The neighbourhood had not changed much but all the children around had obviously grown. A few weeks after returning Jane was rushed to hospital for the birth of our son, Joseph on the 17th July. Since I was not scheduled to return to my teaching duties until the first week of September, I was fortunate both to support Jane and the children during this period and to make the necessary adjustment to life in the U.K. after three years of absence. My return back to teaching at Kirby College was fairly smooth with some new areas of the curriculum being introduced as well as some new personnel. Amy and Esme began their schooling in a first school not far from home. At the end of that transitional year, Jane and I made several major decisions which had long term consequences in terms of our professional and family lives. Jane was eager to recommence her academic studies and with my unqualified support she began her Open University distant learning courses. A little later, I also embarked on an Open University course on Curriculum Design and Development to enable me to understand the theoretical basis of curriculum design but also to further my own education. One significant aspect of Jane's studies with the O.U. was that the first years of her studies also included a week long residential Summer School based at a number of universities around the country. During her first Summer School, I was responsible for a week looking after three very young children on my own. Whilst this was both enjoyable and exhausting, the most interesting thing for me was it raised my awareness that looking after young children meant the lack of adult company, contact and conversations. It was at this point I began to understand some of the additional issues about roles, responsibilities and gender equality.

On the domestic front, we, particularly Jane, were very concerned about Amy's development and behaviour. It was in this context Jane, through our GP contacted a specialist in Neurology in Newcastle. His prognosis was that Amy had suffered brain damage at birth and this would undoubtedly effect her intellectual development and behaviour. Whilst this confirmed our concerns, there were no easy and obvious solutions at hand. In the 1970's, schools were not well equipped to handle children who experienced learning difficulties. Teacher training courses and school were structured around the concept of the average learner and those who did not fit into this pattern were frequently sidelined. On reflection and hindsight, I feel that as a qualified teacher, albeit for older students, I should have taken a more active role in helping with Amy's education in her early years. As Amy grew older embarking on secondary school, and with her siblings 'doing well', her frustration with education and her own limitations resulted in growing behavioural problems later.

A little after a year, we agreed to move to a larger house in Linthorpe, Middlesborough to enable the children to have more individual space. We moved to a large semi-detached house nearer to my place of work. Jane was exceptionally busy at this time, not only was she playing a key role in family life, she was also studying with the Open University. Whilst this occupied a considerable part of her life, she decided to write to the local evening newspaper applying for recipe cards which they were offering to readers. She was then invited to a series of events (preliminary rounds) of a cooking contest. She made it through the preliminary rounds and was invited to participate in the finals. The finals took place on a large stage in a hotel with several hundred people in the audience. There were several contestants and each was supplied with the same mixture of ingredients and they were asked to prepare and cook the meal on stage. The stage was well equipped with the necessary appliances including cookers and the participants were under a time restriction. Note that this was taking place in 1979 long before 'Master Chef' etc. After the cooking was completed and the judges 'did their bit' the contestant who initially entered to acquire a few recipe cards was the winner of this contest. There were several major prizes for the winner including a new cooker for our new home. A few days after the contest, Jane was invited to the Tyne-Tees television studio for an interview. The major and only drawback to Jane winning this contest was that our friends, when invited to dinner parties, had very high expectations. Equally when were invited to their homes, they assumed that we would also have high expectations of what was served.

In addition to acquiring a new cooker, we also decided to equip the kitchen with new units. After purchasing the units and in order to save some money, I decided that I would fit the units myself. The initial task was to remove the old wall units which may have been a few decades old. These were very well installed and deeply embedded in the wall. To remove them, I eventually had to resort to a small sledge hammer which then removed a sizable part of the wall plaster. I eventually cleared the wall units and realised that the whole wall would need to be re-plastered. This was my second big mistake; I decided that I would do this despite having no knowledge or experience of plastering a wall. When I ignorantly commenced on this task, over 90% of the plaster ended up on the floor. After some painstaking and rapid learning, I began to improve and when I eventually completed the task, about 90% was remaining on the wall. Sometime after that difficult learning process, we completed the installation of our new kitchen. Little did we realise at the time that after a few more months in this house we would be moving to West Yorkshire.

Whilst I was pleased that on my return from Zambia I was guaranteed my employment because of conditions of my secondment, I wanted new challenges. This arrived when I was asked to undertake some part time teaching at Teesside Polytechnic (now University of Teesside) during my afternoons off. Lecturers who undertook evening teaching sessions were then allowed an equivalent session off either during the morning or the afternoon. This work was stimulating and very satisfying. After my first year of lecturing at the polytechnic, they offered me extra work in the second year. Since I was timetabled to teach for two evening sessions in the Business Studies Department of Kirby College, I could accommodate this extra teaching during my 'free' sessions. Unfortunately, the management of the Business Studies Department, learning of this, changed my teaching timetable to the extent that I was not able to take any lecturing duties at the polytechnic. This factor convinced me that I would need to apply for a lecturing post elsewhere. I should also mention that in addition to my Open University course which I completed, I was accepted by York University to study for a part time M.A. course in Education commencing in September, 1980. I was extremely fortunate that my first application for a senior lecturer post in business studies resulted in being invited, with several other candidates, in November 1979 for an interview in West Yorkshire. The post was at Shipley College based in the historical village of Saltaire. This was a small College with three relatively small departments and was one of the few colleges in the early 1980's where the Principal was a woman called Barbara Hope. All the different aspects of the interview process went well and at the end of the day, I was offered the post which I readily accepted. The post was scheduled to commence immediately after the Easter vacation.

Saltaire

On returning home, the news was welcomed by all the family. The next few weeks proved to be extremely busy. In addition to work and family life with three young energetic children, Jane and I were both studying Open University courses which left very little time to plan our relocation. We were extremely fortunate that on a Sunday, shortly after I was offered the post at Shipley College, I spotted a friend of ours and his wife in our neighbourhood. We enquired and were informed that they were considering moving to that location and were looking at what was on the housing market there. We informed them that we were in the process of moving and were going to put up our house for sale shortly. They were very interested in this and we showed them around the house. Within a few days, they made us a reasonable offer which we were very happy to accept since this meant that we did not have to go through either an estate agent or the tiresome process of selling the house to a variety of potential buyers. We were then in the process of gradually packing our belongings as well as looking for a property to live in Shipley and surrounding districts. This part of the relocation process was more long drawn out and initially we rented a property for six months in Eccleshill on the outskirts of Bradford. Late in 1980, we moved into a Victorian detached house in Baildon called 'Appletree House' which was our home for the next 16 years.

The first day of working in the Business Studies Department of Shipley College was exciting as well as daunting particularly when my Head of Department informed me that later that day, he would be away for the week on a management residential course and that I would be in charge of the department in his absence. This then was my rapid and steep baptism into educational management. This obviously meant that I had to familiarise myself with the portfolio of courses offered by the department, get to know the different full and part time staff and so on. I was very fortunate that the staff all understood the predicament I was in and they went that extra mile to be helpful. The aspect that concerned me most was that before his departure, Bob also informed me that besides teaching my normal subjects, in two weeks time a new course in the department would begin and I was earmarked to teach this adult class 'Introduction to Information Technology'. Note that in 1980, information technology and computing in Colleges were in their infancy and that my knowledge in this field was a flattering zero. This then was to be my initiation into IT and its application in the world of work. My normal approach to life was and is that all problems have solutions and with this in mind I set about the facing this new challenge. At the weekend, besides purchasing several introductory textbooks on IT, I also purchased a Sinclair ZX80 membrane computer. When I faced this adult class for the first time, I soon learnt that they were also beginning from scratch. This knowledge allowed me to be at least two weeks ahead of the class. When people talk about 'the learning curve', I am certain they do not have this kind of experience in mind. Whilst economics and business studies was still my main teaching focus, this introduction allowed me later to develop a variety of initiatives and courses in the application of IT into the world of work. This period was a very challenging time. In addition to moving house, a new job and new courses to teach, I also began my part time M.A. course at York University which necessitated one evening a week attendance.

Shipley College and particularly the Business Studies Department was also involved in a variety of school linked courses. This initiative was designed to provide young people an opportunity to try out a variety of vocational courses different from the academic curriculum of schools. In some cases, this fairly sound aim was distorted by some schools when they directed young people they found difficult to deal with at school to colleges. At the beginning of the new college year, I was time tabled to teach Commerce to one such group of girls from a variety of local schools. Until then, my teaching experience was completely geared towards the older age range from 16 to 60 years of age. This was a major challenge which necessitated a variety of new teaching strategies and I was pleased to note that several of these young people started their working careers in local building societies and retailing. The other school linked courses I was responsible for were designed for older students who were already in possession of 'O' level (GCSE) qualifications but wished to pursue vocational courses. Many of this cohort subsequently went on to university to pursue degree courses in management, accountancy and law. An amusing incident occurred when David from this group reached 18 years of age. He suggested that as part of his coming of age, he would like to take his class and all his tutors out for a drink at lunch time. Whilst I informed him that although most of the tutors would come to the pub with him, none of us would be drinking any alcohol. As we entered the pub, David was quite vociferous about reaching 18 years of age, and all the tutors and all the students were welcomed by the publican with the exception of David who the publican considered 'under age'. All the other students were amused since some of them were younger than David. After we explained to the publican that David was the host celebrating his 18th birthday he let him in.

One of the tasks I enjoyed was working with colleagues from the other departments of the college on the process of interviewing prospective students applying to the college for the first time. This impartial process allowed prospective students to consider all the different courses before committing themselves to a particular line of study. In addition to the three people from the different departments, the process was supported by the Student Counsellor. This process was a time consuming one since all full time students went through it. I recall one occasion where the interviews took place in an office which had recently undergone some building work and the builders inadvertently left some of their tools behind. After the process was satisfactorily completed with a particular student, I noticed these tools and informed the student that I wanted him to stand up and at that point I gently placed a spirit level on his head, to the bewilderment of my colleagues, and informed him that as he was 'level headed' we would welcome him on his first choice course. I immediately informed him that this was my feeble attempt at humour and he was graceful enough in accepting this. My interviewing colleagues ensured that prior to further interviews, the room was clear of all tempting gadgets, instruments and tools in case I saw them as a further opportunity to use them during the interview process. During the year, every time I came across this student, he always informed me, with a smile on his face, that he was still very level headed.

On the domestic front, Jane was making rapid progress with her Open University degree program and I was completing my part-time M.A. at York University. One of the major problems that arose out of this very demanding time commitment on our part was that the children felt ignored. The children (aged between 6 and 13) were not pleased with this but instead of simply accepting the situation, they drew up placards with a simple message that they wanted more attention from their parents and with these they marched round the dining table at dinner time. This trait of not accepting the conventional, I am pleased to state, remained with Esme and Joseph to this day. Jane and I were obviously shocked by this protest but we recognised the legitimacy of the children's concerns and agreed that, in so far as possible, during either Saturdays or Sundays we would spend time as a family and go out and 'do' something. Jane having completed her graduate studies with the Open University with 'flying colours 'embarked on her PGCE (Post Graduate Certificate in Education) with the intention of teaching in schools. Around that time, I was encouraged by Jane to apply for a part time Tutor Counsellor post with the Open University. Thus in 1983 having completed my course at York University, I began a very stimulating and rewarding part time teaching post with the Open University as a Tutor Counsellor in Social Studies for their Foundation programme.

Working for a little over four years at Shipley College as Senior Lecturer and Deputy Head in the Business Studies Department, I began to consider the opportunities for progressing my career. I initially applied for two Head of Business Studies Department posts and was invited to interviews at both. The first post was at Buxton College in the Derbyshire Dales and the interview process was scheduled over two days. The College structure and the business studies posts were sound and I was fairly positive about the process. Late on the first day, we were informed that besides the role of Head of Department, the post also included supervision of the residential students one night a week which would entail staying on the campus overnight. Having considered this in the context of my lack of experience supervising students in residence and the impact it could have on our family life, I withdrew from the interview process the following day.

Shortly after that I was invited for my second interview for Head of Business Studies Department at a further education college in Cambridge. The process here differed from my first experience since it was divided into two distinct phases: the first phase involved approximately ten 'long listed 'candidates from which a short list of four candidates would be invited the following week for the more formal interviews for the post. After short informal interviews with a variety of senior staff and a narrative about the college from the Principal which included a disgraceful criticism of his predecessor, they informed us that they would be drawing up a shortlist and would inform us of their decision the following day. After all the participants left, I requested a meeting with the Principal. This was arranged and even before I sat down in his office, he intimated that my interviews went very well and he implied that I would be one of the candidates selected for the second and final phase of the interview process. I sat down and calmly informed him that I was withdrawing from this process forthwith which really surprised him. He asked for reasons why I was withdrawing and my calm and collected response was that during his narrative about the college he was very critical of the previous incumbent of the office of Principal, Mr. Hibberd, which I considered unethical particularly as he was not here to either defend or refute the criticisms. Furthermore, I stated that I not only knew the previous Principal but that he was a man who dedicated his life to further the education of young people and a man of total integrity. I also informed him that Mr. Hibberd built the college up from a small further education centre to a sizable college without ever compromising the quality of the provision or losing the full commitment of the staff. He was surprised at my exposition but what really shook him was when I informed him that I knew Mr. Hibberd well and that he was in fact my father-in-law. With the stunned look on his face, I walked out.

Both Mr. and Mrs Hibberd were involved in working for the further education sector in Cambridge for over two decades. Their commitment to the education of young people was inspirational and Mr. Hibberd, despite the managerial and administrative demands of being the head of the institution, continued to teach. On a personal level, my in-laws were very supportive in many ways. They not only encouraged us, as a family, to have our holidays at their cottage in the Yorkshire Dales but also paid for our combined holidays. One such memorable holiday was a coaching holiday to Switzerland in the early 1980's. The holiday was very enjoyable but the thing I remember most vividly from this was that the hotel we stayed in, could not cope with Esme being a vegetarian. The only variant they provided to omelettes was boiled cauliflower. After several complaints, they attempted to vary the menu. These were obviously the early days of their encounter with vegetarians and at the end of our stay, they were gracious enough to apologise and refunded some of the costs.

The other holiday they paid for, which was even more memorable for the wrong reasons, was a joint holiday in Somerset at a residential site where we were accommodated in separate chalets in the summer of 1984. Sometime during the first week after breakfast, I was asked by the site manager to take a phone call from Italy from someone called Andrew. I was puzzled by this and he informed me that the caller specifically asked for me by name. I was anxious and thought that it could be something to do either with a burglary to one of our houses or an accident involving somebody we knew. I answered the phone and learnt that it was Andrew Hook, my sister-in-law, Ann's husband. The news was far worse than anticipated. After a brief conversation and whilst I was immensely taken aback by what he related to me, I gathered my thoughts and proceeded to where the family were still standing around after breakfast. They were all curious about who called and what was the reason for this call. I requested that they all sat down as I had some important news to share. This was the most difficult and excruciating conversation I ever had in my life; I informed them that the phone call was from Andrew and that he had asked me to inform them that their daughter Ann, Jane's sister, had passed away the previous night as a result of a massive brain haemorrhage in Sienna, Italy. We were all in a state of shock at this tragic news and just sat there absorbing the gravity of this information. Shortly after that we began to make hasty preparations to depart and go back to Cambridge. Judith Ann Hook was a gifted scholar working at Aberdeen University as a senior lecturer specialising in Italian history. She was the author of several exceptional books including 'The Sack of Rome' and 'Sienna: A City and its History'. For the latter publication, she was granted the honour of 'A Free Person of Sienna'. Mr. and Mrs. Hibberd were obviously very proud of their daughter and her scholarly work and this tragic news distressed them greatly and all of us immeasurably. Her large funeral in Glasgow was attended by all her academic colleagues from Edinburgh University where she originally worked, from Aberdeen University and Glasgow University where Andrew worked. Whilst we gradually began to come to terms with this premature death, the loss of Judith Ann had grave consequences for her family and particularly her three children.

Returning to my interview for the post in Cambridge and on reflection, perhaps this trait of the arrival 'of a knight in shining armour riding a white stallion' rescuing his/her new organisation from imminent catastrophe is more widespread among CEO's in both the private sector and the public sector than I imagined. Shortly after this experience, it was brought to my notice that Keighley College were advertising for a post for a new Head of Department in Business Studies. Keighley was only 20 minutes drive away from where we lived and that meant that if I was successful in securing the post, we as a family would face no disruption regarding relocation. I applied for the post and I was invited with several other candidates for an interview. I was pleased to be offered the post, which I accepted, commencing on 1st September 1985.

A Brief Digression – The Open University

One of the most significant education initiative introduced by the Labour Government under Harold Wilson, spearheaded by the Education Minister Jennie Lee, was the establishment of the Open University in 1969 and operational since 1971. The main purpose of this was to widen access to higher education to people from all walks of life through innovative distance learning methods offered on a part time basis. In addition to using written material, other means such as radio, TV (now internet) and DVD's were used for many of the programmes. Today the Open University is the biggest provider of undergraduate programmes in Britain. The Social Science Foundation Course which I was involved with included a weekly evening tutorial session as well as a week residential Summer School for the students. These Summer Schools normally took place at a variety of universities during the summer period. My involvement with the Open University as a Tutor Counsellor was one of the most rewarding and invigorating experiences in my teaching career. The students I was involved with over a ten year period were adults from a variety of backgrounds who either missed out on higher education for a variety of reasons or they wished to enhance their professional qualifications further. A small number enrol for the joy of learning. As a Tutor Counsellor I enjoyed working with this cohort of students since they all came from different backgrounds in terms of work and life experiences, I learnt from them about a variety of issues where my own knowledge was either limited or non-existent. Thus whilst I supported their academic aims, they enriched my life with their knowledge and expertise.

I still recall several incidences which had an impact on either my continuous work with the Open University or were personally amusing and enriching. In one of my early years as a Tutor Counsellor, I had a student in my tutorial group called Adrian who was a 'house husband' with health problems. He had just started with the Open University and was struggling with the course. Fortunately the group took the initiative and set up a self help group which met outside the tutorial to deal with their course work and the compulsory tutor marked assignments

(TMA's). As a result, Adrian passed his TMA's but I was obviously concerned for him regarding the external examination which was part of his overall assessment for the course. Following the examination and when the individual students were notified of their respective performance, I occasionally invited them over to my house for an evening buffet. Prior to them arriving, I was sent the full results of my tutorial group and I was very pleased to note that all had passed with several of the students receiving the equivalent of a distinction and many others secured very high marks. However, the thing that pleased me most was that all the students, arriving before Adrian asked me about his performance rather than anything about the 'high flyers'. Without exception, they were all delighted when I informed them that Adrian had passed. The significant of this was that the group had gelled and supported each other and were more concerned about their weakest member of the group than the high flyers.

One of the most enjoyable and invigorating experience of a Tutor Counsellor is to be part of two one week teaching/learning sessions at the annual Summer Schools which took place at a variety of university campuses around the country. I particularly looked forward to this because on becoming a senior member of the college management team, I was requested not to take any teaching duties at the college. The Summer Schools offered me the opportunity to cast aside my role playing persona and simply enjoy teaching and tutoring an enthusiastic group of adult students who also enjoyed the social atmosphere of Summer School. On one such occasion at Keele

University, two fellow tutors, a group of about eight students and I went out to an Italian restaurant in Stoke for an evening meal. As we entered, I took the head waiter to one side and informed him that it was one of the mature student's birthday and could they do something to surprise him. He was pleased to inform me that would be no trouble. Once we finished our main course, the lights went out and one of the waiters with a guitar started singing a happy birthday song whilst another waiter brought out a small cake with lit sparklers on it. Frank, to say he was 'gob smacked' would be understating the expression on his face but he gathered himself quickly and gracefully thanked the waiters for this wonderful surprise. They in turn, informed him that it was a pleasure and informed him that I was the person who informed them. Once the waiters were out of earshot, he informed the group that it was not his birthday at all but he played along not to disappoint the waiters. But he also informed me that whilst this was an enjoyable surprise, there would be retribution of an equivalent kind. On the Thursday evening of Summer School, usually there was the Summer School Ball/Dance which was attended by most of the students and staff, around four hundred plus. On this Thursday, half way through the evening, the compere asked for silence for an important announcement and as the hall grew silent he announced that Ahmed, the Social Science Tutor and Anita, one of the students would like to announce their engagement. He proceeded to ask that the dance floor be cleared and for Ahmed and Anita to lead off the next dance. I meekly complied since Anita was well briefed by Frank, she joined in this. After the dance was completed and I walked around the hall, I was congratulated by many students and fellow tutors. It took some explaining to my colleagues that I was happily married and this was a just a small and amusing retribution from Frank.

On another memorable occasion I was working at Sterling University and after the full day of teaching and socialising with the adult students and staff, we all retired for the night to our respective rooms in the skyscraper residential block. At around two a.m. in the morning the piercing fire alarm rang out and within a few minutes all the students and staff descended into the safe zone. One of my students, an elderly woman named Claire who was a retired professional, came up to me still in her dressing gown asked me where was the fire? After making some enquiries, I reassured her that it was a false alarm and that she did not have to worry about anything. She assured me that she was not really worried and proceeded to inform me that even if it was real fire and she lost all her clothes, shoes and jewellery in the room it would not bother her, and clutching some papers to her chest, she stated that she brought out her most valuable possession – her TMA (Tutor Marked Assignment) which she needed to submit for her assessment. This inspiring episode encouraged me to continue working for the Open University for a few more years than I originally intended to.

CHAPTER NINE

ONWARDS AND UPWARDS

Having spent five very satisfying and productive years as senior lecturer at Shipley College, I was ready to face a fresh academic challenge as Head of the Business Education Department at Keighley College. The College was a more traditional technical college with a sizable department of engineering as well as a department for the building industry and a large general education department. The Principal, Doug Hardaker, was also relatively new and he was very supportive. The other striking feature of the college was that almost all the senior and middle managers were male, a common feature of the traditional technical colleges in the 1980's and early 1990's. The presence of only male middle managers in my new department was further reinforced by some of the male members through their perceptions of the role they were expected to play in the department. A significant amount of the work involved delivering secretarial courses to young people and adults on a full time and part time basis predominantly by female staff, yet there were no female managers of any significance. As the department grew, I had the opportunity to advertise for a new senior lecturer post and I took this opportunity to redress this imbalance by advertising this senior lecturer post in secretarial studies. This initiative was obviously welcomed by the secretarial staff but shortly after the advertisement was placed in the press, I had a stream of male middle managers suggesting that I had put their career progression in jeopardy since they were not able to meet the specifications for the job. I took their concerns seriously but explained to them, supported by statistical evidence, why I made the decision.

At home, Jane was making rapid progress with her career as a teacher. Amy was growing up rapidly and struggling with her education at school in the 1980's environment where there was very little understanding of the learner support required to assist young people with learning difficulties. Her siblings, Esme and Joseph, were making excellent progress in school. Amy's growing frustration resulted in behavioural problems. Whilst initially her problems were centred on home life, as she grew older they began to turn to mixing with 'bad' company. On reflection, I now wonder if I fully understood Amy's problems then, and would I would have handled it differently if I had, and would it have resulted in a different outcome for Amy? Perhaps this feeling of guilt that one of your children had a difficult adolescence and young adulthood is one that persists for a very long time regardless of your role or outcome.

One of the big advantages of being a new Head of Department was that this offered me an opportunity to explore new areas of work for the department. I was very fortunate that at that time, the regional office of Government in Leeds was financially supporting new educational initiatives in Colleges. With the information I gathered from my eldest brother being a doctor and my growing enthusiasm about computer technology and its potential in administrative work, we put forward a proposal to introduce and improve the use of computers in doctors' surgeries. It is worth pointing out that in the mid 1980's very few surgeries nationally were using computers in their surgeries. Our pioneering submission was accepted and the initiative soon drew the attention of a multinational computer company and a major university. In simple terms, the initiative involved training surgery staff to use computers for recording patient data as well as carrying out normal administrative tasks. In the context of today, this would appear as routine work practice, but in the 1980's very few surgeries used data processing to keep records and most medical staff were computer illiterate. At this time, another initiative I was particularly interested in was employment, or lack of, employment opportunities for young Black and Asian people in Keighley and surrounding districts. Working with the local authority, I succeeded in securing funding for a project called 'Black and Highly Visible' which ensured that young Black and Asian people in work and training were seen in frontline positions thereby acting as role models for their peers as well as getting the host communities used to the perception that these young people could, and were, contributing to society. This initiative was moderately successful but only had a very small time span. Unfortunately, the problem of unemployment among young Black and Asian people still persists today in all parts of the country.

After two reasonably successful years as Head Of Business Education, structural changes in the College were necessary because of the departure of two Heads of Departments. The Principal and Governors agreed on a major structural change by creating a small number of Faculties and two Vice Principals posts. A number of my colleagues encouraged me to apply for the posts and after two and half years as Head of Department, I secured the post of Vice Principal, Resources. The other post, Vice Principal, Academic was secured by Graham Packham. Over the next seven years we worked together effectively on a significant number of college related issues. The role of Vice Principal – Resources meant that in addition to being responsible for the use of college buildings and resources within them, the remit included responsibility for the college library, health and safety, oversight of the technician services, coordinating and applying for external funding, sharing joint responsible for strategic planning, responsibility for marketing, for computing resources and, like the Home Office, responsibility for anything that did not fit in to the academic remit.

The remit also allowed me to seek and secure external funding for specific projects. The two projects that I initiated during this early period both involved addressing issues faced by the Black and Asian communities. The first one involved the difficulties experienced by Black and Asian graduates in securing employment appropriate to their qualification and knowledge. We identified that one of the weakness of their applications was the lack of relevant 'hands on experience'. With this in mind, we secured funding for a short term project for placing unemployed Black and Asian graduates in work placement in a variety of business organisations in the district – nowadays this may be termed as 'internship'. Then this was relatively new and it was moderately successful since a number of employers subsequently informed us that their perception of Black and Asian graduates changed significantly for the positive. The other project which I initiated, but subsequently delegated to the Faculty of Business and General Education, involved encouraging the Asian business community in Keighley to widen their business expectation away from 'the corner shop' and consider diversifying to other sectors of the economy. One element of this initiative was taking a number of Keighley Asian business people for two days, to visit the thriving and diversified Birmingham Asian business community. The trip included visiting a variety of small manufacturing and assembling companies as well as listening to their owners about how they diversified and expanded. This aspiration-raising attempt was moderately successful and on returning to Keighley, this information was passed on to other members of the business community who were unable to attend, at the Keighley Asian Business Forum meeting of which I was a member. During the first few years, I began to develop my management skills in a direction I never anticipated when going into lecturing. Whilst I was in full time employment at the college, I continued working for the Open University on a part time basis, in my own time.

Thus I was able to continue to do what I found most rewarding, be engaged in teaching enthusiastic adults at least once a week and for two weeks at Summer School.

After a little less than two years as Vice Principal, I decided to 'test the waters' regarding Principal posts. I made two applications for Principal's posts at two different colleges in Leicestershire. Both these colleges were absorbed or merged with other colleges in more recent years. I was surprised to be invited for interviews for both posts. The first post was located in a medium sized college in an industrial area of Leicestershire. The interviews were scheduled over two days in April 1989 and commenced with a long list of candidates on the first day and narrowed down to three candidates for the second day. I was pleasantly surprised to be asked to return for the second day. The panel consisted of five Governors of the college and three senior local authority officers including the Director of Education acting in an advisory capacity. I thought my personal interview went reasonably well, considering this was my first interview for a Principal's post. After all three candidates were interviewed, the panel took some considerable time debating and discussing what they perceived as the strengths and weaknesses of each of the candidates. At the end of their deliberations, the internal candidate was offered and accepted the post. A senior advisor informed me that several members of the panel thought my interview went well and I was the 'runner up' and wished me good fortune for future applications and interviews for the post of Principal. I was relatively pleased with the outcome, considering this was my first interview for the most senior post at a reasonable size college. This, however, was not the end of this matter. The second interview for the Principal's post was in a relatively small college in a small town in Leicestershire and after the first day, I withdrew my application since I did not see this as a sufficiently challenging role.

After about two weeks, I was surprised to receive a letter from the Race Equality Commission informing me that a Governor and member of the interview panel had lodged a complaint that when the panel were making their decision regarding who should be offered the post of Principal at the College, certain members of the panel, he felt, made discriminating remarks about my candidature. I was asked about my opinion regarding the possibility of a formal investigation. My response was that I was unable to comment on 'what went on behind closed doors' but if a formal complaint was made, then the Commission should proceed with their enquiry and keep me informed.

In June 1991, the Commission for Racial Equality published its report of what occurred during the appointment process for the post of Principal of Hinckley College, Leicestershire entitled 'A Question of Merit'. In addition to the report, the Commission sent me revealing details of what took place in the final selection process for the post of Principal, much of which was not published in the final report. According to this secondary report, three of the Governors favoured my appointment, all the Council officers were in agreement with that, whilst two of the Governors favoured the internal candidate. At this point, the two Governors who were in favour of the internal candidate asked the Governor, who was also the Chair of the panel, to withdraw from the room to have a private discussion, in contravention of the normal interview process. When the panel reconvened, the Chair changed her mind, with no explanation, and used her casting vote in favour of the internal candidate.

It is interesting to note that during the Commission's investigation, the Chair's affidavit said "Candidate B (me) also interviewed well but tended to talk about educational concepts during his interview, rather than the practicalities of the job". This statement, however, the Commission found contradicted the Governor's interview record. Under **Application,** she had written "Excellent, clear grasp of what is expected of a Principal and the future development of a College". Under the heading **Curriculum,** she noted "Good experience of curriculum work and the importance of entitlement curriculum". Under **Staff Development**, she had noted " Strong and practical interest in staff development and appraisal". Under **Communication**, she noted "full appreciation of the need for close links with other institutions and gave innovative examples". Under **Resources,** she noted "Particularly well versed in resources and technology". Under **Community,** she wrote "concern for the community and its needs". Under **Professional commitment/Personal,** she wrote "A very committed and professional person with drive and energy; would contribute to educational thinking". With this evidence, the Commission found that the Chair of the panel was not telling the truth about my performance at interview and they concluded that the true reason for not appointing me was that I was an Asian. As well as this unfortunate episode, the Commission reported that when short listing for the Principal's post at Melton College of Further Education, a Governor objected to the appointment of an Asian. Since I withdrew from the interview process for this post after the first day for a variety of reasons, the Governor's objection did not apply. These two instances clearly indicated that whilst the majority of Governors were open minded and objective in their work as college governors, there was still a minority with deep rooted prejudice against Black and Asian professionals in Colleges.

One positive outcome from this report, was that it gave impetus to Colleges to adopt and publicise their respective equal opportunity policy as well as ensure that there was adequate training available for Governors and potential Governors on their roles and responsibilities regarding equal opportunities. Whilst this was positive, the account of what went on behind the scenes and the possibility of racial discrimination had the negative effect of putting me off from applying for the post of Principal for a number of years.

After a few years, I began to apply for the post of Principal at a variety of Colleges, excluding London since I had no desire to live there. I was invited to a number of Colleges for an interview and the usual format was the interviews were conducted over two days and by the second day the long list was reduced to about three candidates. This allowed me to develop my interview skills further but there were occasions when I felt that my performance was very poor and I would find it difficult to appoint myself to the posts. There were, however, many other occasions where I progressed to the second day but withdrew because, having previously researched the location and its economic and social environment, I felt that the position did not provide me with the kind of challenge I expected. There may have been two other occasions when I suspected an element of discrimination took place. In one incident, the recruitment was carried out by a reputable national company and prior to going on a short vacation, I phoned them up to ascertain the progress of my application. A manager handling this process informed me that I was one of the top three applicants they would be recommending to the Governors for interview and appointment. On my return from the short vacation, I contacted the company to seek further information regarding this post of Principal. The same manager informed me that, despite their recommendation, the governors did not wish to include me on the shortlist for interview because they felt 'he would not fit in'? I was unable to pursue this further since I was unable to gather any further information from the company responsible for the recruitment process. The other incident of possible discrimination occurred when I progressed with two other candidates to the final selection process. The two senior local authority officers present as advisors at interview, suggested that I was the 'best candidate' for the post but the governors decided to offer the post to the internal 'white' candidate. In this particular situation, to the best of my knowledge, no formal complaints were made and the local authority officer who informed me of the outcome did not wish to pursue this further. The postscript to this was that after less than two years into the post coupled to a very poor inspection report, the appointee was dismissed.

By the late 1980's, Amy had left school and was taking a first level course at College in Caring and her tutors spoke well of her progress. Esme had secured a place at Birmingham University and Joseph was making excellent progress at his upper school. Every few weeks, early on Saturday mornings, Joseph and I would go to the wholesale market to purchase boxes of fruit which would be stored in our large basement. Joseph was developing a sharp wit and I recall that once shopping at Asda in the late 1980's, we purchased a few loose over ripe and wrinkly passion fruit . When we arrived at the checkout, the young person operating the checkout was not familiar with this purchase and asked what was this. Before I said a word, Joseph's instant reply was 'Dried up scrotum of a Mountain Goat'. The innocent checkout operator then proceeded to look at the provisions check list provided by Asda for Joseph's colourful description of passion fruit. At this point I interjected and informed the operator that it was commonly called 'passion fruit'.

At this time, Jane was making excellent progress in her career securing the post of Deputy Head and Head of a primary school in a very short space of time. In terms of family life and my own career, I should have taken greater note of a remark made by one of my nephews in Manchester during one of our visits, when he stated that every time we met,

I talked a lot about work and very little else. On reflection, this passing remark perhaps summarised my preoccupation with work and the lack of a work/life balance. My involvement with organisations in the community grew and besides the Keighley Asian Business Forum, I was also a primary school governor, a Company Secretary for a training company associated with the College, a member of Town Centre Management Group, and a board member of the Keighley Council for Voluntary Services. Besides the fortnightly summer vacation and the week we usually spent in the Yorkshire Dales and getting together during the festive season in the late 1980's and early 1990's there were very few things we did as a family then. Perhaps this was the beginning either of the family growing apart or the children carving up their own paths, whatever it was, this was very different from the close knit family I grew up in. On reflection, my preoccupation with work may have contributed to the growing gap in my relationship with Jane. Perhaps my lack of awareness and poor emotional intelligence may have contributed to further problems in our family relationship.

Much of our tensions centred around Amy's inability to keep her room tidy and my growing frustration with this situation. The only other minor incident that comes to mind occurred in the mid 1990's a couple of days after most of the festive season visitors departed. Besides Jane and the family, we had Esme's friend, Arthur, still with us. In my opinion, Arthur was an irresponsible, disruptive but likable rogue. His partner and mother of their child had recently broken off their relationship because of his irresponsible behaviour. Early in the morning Amy informed me that during the night Arthur tried to 'jump' into bed with her and she told him to remove himself from her room. Very shortly after the conversation with Amy, Jane had a word with me with a query of whether, Arthur now homeless, could live with us since we had a spare room. My unequivocal response to this was 'NO'. I strongly believed then that his presence in our household would be very disruptive and the little things that were holding the family together would quickly evaporate. I assumed that this information was then conveyed to Esme.

Sometime later that morning, we were all in the kitchen and Joseph went for some fresh air through the kitchen door. Arthur immediately bolted the door and Joseph was locked out. Joseph's immediate response was hard and well aimed kick to the door which had the effect of breaking the bolt. My immediate and shocked response was 'this is totally unacceptable behaviour', knowing that this was another unnecessary repair for me to undertake, but aimed at no one in particular. I was surprised that at this juncture Esme stridently stated words to the effect 'You should not talk to my friends like that!' She proceeded to her room and packed her bag and left home with Arthur in tow. I was told subsequently that after a few days with friends, she had returned to Birmingham where she was attending University. I was surprised by her reaction but I was equally surprised when Jane also packed her bag and drove off in her car, without a word to me. After two days, Jane returned and informed me that she went to her parents holiday cottage in the Dales. Very little was said about the incident and our, now relatively different relationship, continued and my belief was that both Esme and Jane were disappointed with my negative reaction to the prospect of Arthur living with us. It is also very likely that they were both more sympathetic to Arthur's plight and more charitable about his behaviour than I was.

In the meantime, Joseph applied to the University of Cambridge to study physics and mathematics. They accepted him provisionally on the condition that he achieved passes in two 'special papers' in his 'A' level exams. Shortly after that, during a parents and teachers meeting, Joseph's class tutor explained Joseph's progress to me and he stated that his teachers in physics and mathematics had gone through all the past special exam papers with him and Joseph completed all of these very satisfactorily. There was little else they could do. I informed the teachers they should not worry about this and if Joseph succeeded in his 'A' levels , including the Special Papers, I wouldn't blame them for this. I think it took them a few minutes to digest this light hearted remark and eventually began to smile. In the event, Joseph not only succeeded in achieving the 'A' level grades including the Special Papers, he exceeded the conditional grades. Prior to Joseph going to university, he saved a reasonable sum of money to purchase a small car, with some assistance from Jane and me. He had previously passed his driving test and whilst driving one Saturday on the moor road to Ilkley, he capsized the car on an awkward bend. The police 'phoned me at home, Jane was working in the local Oxfam shop at the time, to inform me of the incident as well as where this took place and asked me to pick up Joseph from there. On arrival, I proceeded to the ambulance where Joseph was sitting and he began to explain to me what transpired, but he was surprised that I was not too interested in that and was more interested in his well being than all else. The paramedic explained to me that besides the shock, there did not appear to be any visible injuries. Furthermore, he informed me that after the car capsized, Joseph crawled out of the car shaken but obviously not hurt. With a smile on his face, the paramedic also informed me that after Joseph evacuated the car, he became aware that he left the radio on which was still blaring out music. Realising this, Joseph crawled back into the capsized car and switched the radio off. The car was insured but was a 'write off'. We were all thankful that this learning experience did not result in any injuries. This incident also confirmed that Joseph was a 'completer/finisher 'which necessitated switching off the radio. At the end of that academic year, Amy completed her course and the feedback from her work placements were all very positive. Esme completed her studies at Birmingham with a very good degree, and Joseph was about to commence his undergraduate studies in Cambridge.

The early 1990's witnessed a profound shift in the structure and organisation of the further education sector nationally when under a Conservative Government Colleges of Further Education were separated from local authority control and became incorporated bodies overseen by Further Education Funding Council (FEFC) a Quango. This profound change gave enterprising colleges freedom and opportunities to develop new provision to meet the skills and challenges brought about by the rapidly changing economic and social environment. It also allowed colleges to restructure their respective management and educational operations. In my personal opinion, the most regrettable provision of these structural and organisational changes was the introduction of Remuneration Committees to determine the pay of Principal and senior staff. This phenomena was also introduced to other public sector organisations such as the Health Service, Universities, Local Authorities, etc. The overall effect of this particular change was/is the growing disparity of pay between the CEO and Senior staff of these organisations and front line staff responsible for delivering the service. Prior to this change, the pay ratio between front line full time staff and CEO's was in the region 1 to 3, this ratio now is in the region of 1 to 5 and in some cases 1 to 8. I will comment further on this profound change on the ethos of public service and the effect it has had.

One of the other major changes affecting Colleges at that time was the introduction of a more rigorous inspection system. Keighley College was one of the early colleges to be inspected. Whilst guidelines were published, we underestimated the very detailed scrutiny the academic work of the college was going to be experiencing. The published post inspection report was highly critical of a variety of curriculum areas. Whilst my role as Vice Principal – Resources was minimal in the process, I was nevertheless very concerned about the issues raised. This report obviously had major implications regarding the future of the college and it required a detailed response in terms planning and actions to be taken to address the weaknesses identified. The Principal, I assume with the support of the Chair of Governors, engaged a firm of consultants (one of the 'Big Four' involved with the Further Education sector) to carry out an audit of the management of the college and particularly of its academic work. The consultants interviewed all the senior managers and a significant number of middle managers. The confidential report given to the Principal and Chair of Governors had profound implications in terms of the structure and organisation of the senior management team.

During one of our normal Senior Management meetings involving the Principal, the two Vice Principals and Heads of Faculties, the Principal asked Graham, the Vice Principal – Academic, to join him in his office for a private word. He was informed that he had an hour to collect his personal belongings from his office and he would be escorted out of the building by a security officer. A short time after that we learnt what occurred and to say that 'I was shocked 'is a gross understatement of my feelings then. I was aware that Graham was unhappy working with the Principal and he would have accepted a negotiated severance package and left without the indignity and anguish. Since I worked reasonably closely with Graham on overlapping issues, I felt that his treatment was unjustified and a more diplomatic solution would have resulted in a similar outcome with little difference in the financial cost to the college. Shortly after this event, at the weekend, I wrote the following verse:

Faceless men behind closed doors
Blame, Judge, and Condemn
Hearing one side of a many sided story
No Crime, No Misconduct, No misdemeanours
No Negligence, No Incompetence
Perhaps a case of mistaken identity?
This is your sentence, there is no appeal !
You have sixty minutes !
Pack your possessions !
No time for farewells !
You will be escorted out by a warden !
Have we not been here before, another time,
    another place?

I was not troubled by the decision of the Governing body, since they had the authority to hire and fire senior staff, but by the manner this was executed. Before this event, I was very reasonably content with working at Keighley College and for several years prior to that I stopped making applications for other posts. This traumatic event simply ignited my desire to move and seek to work elsewhere.

Jane, understanding my grave concerns suggested that I could consider early retirement as an option and that she would keep her headship and support the household. Her generous offer whilst tempting, as this was, I did not consider to be a realistic option for me since I felt I could continue to make a contribution to further education and informed Jane that I would be applying for posts elsewhere. I immediately began the process of seeking a new post and applied for three posts – one for a Vice Principal in a Somerset College and two Principals' posts. I was invited for interview to all three Colleges. The Vice Principal's post was my first interview and at the end of day one, the Principal and Chair of Governors had a private conversation with me. At this informal meeting they informed me that I did well on the first stage but suggested that with my experience and qualifications, I should not be applying for Vice Principal's posts but for a Principal's post in further education colleges. I took the eminently sensible and helpful advice and withdrew. Very shortly after that I was invited for an interview for a Principal's post at a Nottinghamshire college of further education.

CHAPTER TEN

THE ROBIN HOOD COUNTRY

I was invited for interview for the post of Principal at South Nottingham College and it was scheduled to last over three days, commencing Thursday 11 July 1996. The process was similar to other senior post interviews in that the first day comprised a long list of candidates which was reduced after the first day, to a short list of candidates for the second day of interviews. The difference at South Nottingham College was the short list was further reduced for the third day and the central focus here was to make a presentation to the Board of Governors on specific issues which were given to the remaining three candidates at the end of the second day. Needless to say, I was fortunately selected for both the short list and for a formal presentation to the Governors on Saturday 13 July 1996. After having two intensive days of interviews and testing, I was pleased to be selected for the final day. Once we were issued with the topics for the next day, I drove back home to West Yorkshire and prepared my presentation. The presentations were scheduled to commence at 9.00 a.m. and with my surname beginning with 'C' I was conscious that I would be the first of the three candidates to be called.

My presentation to the Governors went as planned and I strolled out of the building to get some fresh air. As I walked around the premises approaching the car park, I was buttonholed by two smartly dressed gentlemen who asked me 'are you joining us?' I was surprised and assumed that they were members of staff of South Nottingham College and replied that there were still two other candidates making their presentation and then there would be some time before a decision was reached. The two gentlemen repeated the question of whether I was going to join them. I soon realised that there seemed to be some misunderstanding and that there may be two separate things taking place in the vicinity. I should point out that the campus site was shared between the College and an upper school. I enquired about what it was I was being asked to join them in? They informed me that they were using the West Bridgford School's swimming pool for baptising new members of the Seventh Day Adventist Church and they were welcoming the new recruits and guiding them to the location of the swimming pool. I wondered was this an omen or just a coincidence ? I informed the two gentlemen of the reason for my presence on the site and they wished me good fortune.

The two other candidates completed their respective presentations and after the governors spent some time discussing the three candidates' presentations as well as the two previous days' interview process, I was requested to return to the room where the presentation took place. The Chair of Governors, Bernard Rutter, informed me that they had reached a decision and offered me the post of Principal of South Nottingham College, which I accepted. I also informed them that whilst I would be making several visits to the College before my starting date, I was obliged to give two months notice to my present college employers. At my first Association of College's Conference I was approached by a representative from one of the colleges and he enquired if I was the first Asian College Principal? I was surprised by the question and replied that 'Asian Principals normally live and work in Asia' but I quickly reassured him that I may have been the person he was looking for but that 'I was the first Principal appointed in the UK who comes from an Asian Heritage background'. Fortunately he understood what I was implying and then we proceeded to talk about the educational issues we then collectively faced in the college sector. I still sometimes wonder, whether joining the Seven Day Adventist Church would have been an easier option than being a Principal of a large further education college.

On returning home, the family were pleased for me but it presented a logistic location problem. Since all the 'children' had either left home or lived in a hall of residence (Joseph at Cambridge University), Appletree House was going to be a large house with only one person living in it during week days, after I commenced my post in Nottingham. Since Jane was then a Head Teacher at a large first school in Leeds, it seemed appropriate that we considered selling Appletree House and purchasing two smaller properties, one in Leeds and one in Nottingham. This process obviously took some time but eventually we secured two reasonable comfortable houses one in Leeds and the other in West Bridgford, Nottingham.

Prior to taking up my post in October, I planned several visits to South Nottingham College to begin the process of building up a more comprehensive picture of my new working environment, determining the obvious strengths of the organisation and the obvious areas which may require development. At the end of August, the College organised an 'Open Day' for advising and recruiting students, including adults, for the next academic year which commenced in mid September. Since my appointment was in July and many of the teaching staff were on vacation then, I was not a recognisable face to many of them. I made this unannounced visit on a Saturday morning and was delighted by the reception. The staff on duty welcomed me as a prospective new student. I was offered appropriate guidance for an adult student returning to further his studies. At the end of the process, I informed the now bemused staff that I was very pleased by their approach to prospective new students and that I was their newly appointed Principal. I was very pleased with my visit to the College and the staff's caring and sensitive approach in the recruitment process.

I was given a memorable Leaving Party by my colleagues at Keighley College and I informed them that there were occasions in life when one had to leave a place where work was once fulfilling and enjoyable but changed circumstances coupled to what I perceived as an injustice to a colleague, I sincerely felt that I had no other option, but to leave.

I took up my appointment as Principal of South

Graham presenting me with the gift from the staff of Keighley College

Nottingham College on 1 October 1996. I was welcomed by the senior staff and the two Personal Assistants (P.A's) in the senior staff office. Linda and Azmina were the two P.A's. and over the next six and half years, I built up a strong bond with both of them and they were always very supportive. Linda, my personal P.A. was an excellent gate keeper and particularly when managers wished to see me to plead for more resources, her standard response was 'Can you demonstrate that what you are asking for will result in direct benefits for the students'. If the answer was either vague or negative she would inform the manager that she/he was wasting their time meeting with the Principal since he would ask you the same question.

On my second week in post, I was presented with my first major problem where a quick decision was required. The problem concerned the senior computer technician and the issue was regarding downloading and storing sexual images of children on a college computer. The issue was brought to our notice by a fellow computer technician. My response to this was that I asked a senior member of staff to immediately determine the veracity of this information and report to me as soon as possible. After this was confirmed, I issued instructions that the senior technician be suspended forthwith and the police be informed of this transgression. The senior management team discussed this event and agreed that the perpetrator be dismissed but unfortunately he resigned before I could sack him. The individual was subsequently tried and, I believe, was given a short custodial sentence. The more disturbing part of this baptism by fire was that I was informed later by a couple of members of staff that he baby sat for them.

Sometime shortly after taking up my post, I embarked on writing a detailed criticism of the dismissal of my colleague at Keighley College for publication in the Keighley News. I strongly felt that an injustice was perpetrated and that the Principal and Governors could have handled this whole episode more sensitively with possibly the same outcome. I informed my chair of governors of what I was doing and he was very supportive. The detailed analysis of what took place and roles and responsibilities of various people was published and it created a minor ripple both in Keighley and the further education world. This exercise, perhaps enabled me to banish another one of my demons and move on.

In the following summer, Amy got married to Christopher Graver and sometime later, she gave birth to a son called Adam. Their relationship started well but Amy experienced health difficulties early on and this persisted for several years. We were both supportive but Jane was closer at hand and frequently baby sat for them. Christopher was the main carer for Adam and they developed a strong bond between them. Unfortunately the relationship came under increasing stress and eventually Amy and Christopher separated. After a difficult and prolonged family court hearing, Amy and Adam lived with Jane in Cambridge. After several years, Jane and Amy agreed that it would be in Adam's long term interest if went to live with Christopher who was now living in Peterborough. One of the distressing part of family life during the late 1990's was the death of both of Jane's parents through illness. I was particularly saddened by the death of Mr. Hibberd since he was one of my career role models. On reflection, I think my preoccupation with work contributed significantly to my eventual marriage breakdown. In addition, perhaps, my time frozen cultural expectations of marriage and family life played an equally large part in this.

Unlike many 'new brooms' taking up posts of CEO's, I was determined to avoid making sweeping structural changes to the organisation without understanding the underlying strengths and potential of the existing staff and where there were gaps and identified areas for further development. I set about this task, over the first few months, by drawing up a management audit form and interviewing all senior and middle managers at the college. Most of the interviews lasted an hour but some went beyond that. This was a wonderful opportunity for me, primarily to listen to the views of my new colleagues, determine their respective strengths, their potential for further development and their individual perception of progress and possible growth of the college. This exercise was informative and rewarding. I also made a detailed analysis of the student profile of the college and this revealed that the college was heavily engaged in 'franchising' its work to other bodies such as the British Canoe Union, other sporting organisations nationally and other regional and local organisations. This franchising work accounted for nearly 30,000 students and for a significant part of the college budget. Unfortunately, I also inherited a large financial deficit which we collectively turned into a relatively healthy surplus in a very short space of time.

This detailed work allowed me to make a presentation to the Governors regarding the necessary changes required to ensure that the college had a sound financial base as well as to reduce its very heavy dependence on franchising courses to other organisations nationally. I also advocated that there would be a need to make some structural changes, driven by my belief that the central focus of the college should be teaching and learning offered to locally based students. The Governors were very supportive and this enabled me to make the changes to senior management team by appointing the Assistant Principal – Curriculum & Student Support to the position of Deputy Principal. My reason for doing this was simple – to enhance and emphasise the role of teaching and learning. I was very fortunate in that two of the senior managers, Annie White and Mary Robson, were exceptionally good at their respective posts – teaching & learning and human resources. I frequently depended on their diplomatic skills and emotional intelligence in dealing with difficult situations. I was also pleased to learn that several of the middle managers were equally good at what they did and had great potential for further development- John, Student Centre Manager, Sarah and Yvonne, Service Industries, Alan in Art & Design and Jean, Adult Education were exceptional. I also begun to be aware of the very high quality of teaching and support staff right across the college. This was reassuring and provided me with the opportunity to lead a very successful college by making some the necessary changes to go further. One area I identified early on was the weakness in marketing of the college and we appointed an excellent Marketing Manager to promote the college locally and begin the process of recruiting more full time and part time students locally and gradually reduce our heavy dependence on franchised work. The detailed 'needs analysis' and the college's Strategic Plan were accepted by the Governors and this clearly indicated the direction the college was going in and all members of staff were made aware of this.

One of the early changes I instigated was a result of a visit I made to the Community Centre in Cotgrave. Cotgrave was an old coal mining location and the college used the centre to provide adults with opportunities for training and retraining in vocational education. One aspect that disturbed me on this visit to the Cotgrave Community Centre was the state of the computers the students were taught to use – they were outdated and the software used was also outdated. I informed the Centre Manager that the College would replace the hardware & software very shortly since I firmly believed that disadvantaged communities should not be further disadvantaged by being taught on outdated technology. The Manager and the students were surprised and pleased that their opportunities to improve their chances of employment was enhanced.

During the summer vacation, I began the process of ensuring that we made physical changes to the learning environment. One of the most disturbing visual aspect of the college environment was that almost all the college's interior walls were covered by posters and leaflets and most were unrelated to the college. My first instruction to all staff was that, after cleaning up and repainting all the walls of the main building, the only notices and posters that would go up would be in designated glass display boxes. Having done that, I then set about securing funds from the Further Education Funding Council (FEFC), supported by a bank loan of £2.5m, to enhance and improve the learning environment for students and staff. The loan was secured and payments were scheduled over 10 years. By planning and controlling income and expenditure, without any effect on students and staff, we were able to pay back the loan in 18 months. At around that time, the Chair of Governors resigned because of additional senior responsibilities in his own work and was replaced by Kevin Shine. The new Chair and I built up a very good working relationship and he was very supportive regarding the strategic direction the college was attempting to achieve. I believe that the impact of this change in the learning environment was a positive one on staff morale and student learning. Around that time, when talking to one of the Governors, he posed an interesting question to me, in the context of England playing South Africa at cricket: he asked 'I know you come from South Africa and England are playing them in a cricket test, who do you support?' I think my reply surprised him – I stated that I support Yorkshire, then Nottinghamshire, then England and then South Africa, in that order. Furthermore, I stated that the reason for this ranking was that all three of my children were born in Yorkshire and I spent most of my working life in different parts of Yorkshire and besides that Yorkshire and Nottinghamshire play very attractive cricket. In terms of England, I support them over South Africa since I spent most of my life living, studying and working in England and I have a great affinity to the country. I think he was surprised and even pleased with my fulsome answer.

An interesting development that occurred locally , at that time, was the merger of two further education colleges and a sixth form college which gave rise to a very large college – 'New College, Nottingham'. This merger had the effect of creating some restlessness among the other remaining colleges in Nottingham, particularly colleges close to the city centre. Encouraged by the funding council, a meeting was convened by the other four remaining colleges and the remaining sixth form college to consider the possibility of a further merger. The Principals of the colleges including me, had several long meetings to discuss this possibility. Being the 'new boy on the block', I sat and listened attentively to my colleagues talking about the merger predominantly from a personal interest view. After several of these meetings, I elaborated on my position – I informed my colleagues that what I observed during these meetings disturbed me enormously, since not a single reference was made to either the curriculum or the benefits the students would experience from this proposed merger and the talks centred predominantly around the role each of them wished to play in the proposed merger. I further informed, my now surprised colleagues, that as the Principal of the largest college in the group, I was withdrawing from these discussions. Shortly after that the talks of merger between the colleges was abandoned.

The positive groundwork in teaching, learning and self improvement coupled to the improved learning environment meant that when we were inspected in late 1998, the staff and college were well prepared to face the challenge. The inspection carried out in November resulted in our 'Learning and Teaching' grades for 'Outstanding' and 'Good' quality graded as the third highest in the country with only one Further Education College and one Sixth Form College achieving better grades. At the time of inspection, there were over 450 colleges and our overall grade was a tribute to the excellent work done by the staff of the college and particularly Annie White, the Lead Person for the college and her team. The changes we made were recognised by the inspectors when they stated 'There is an open, accessible and consultative management style. The management team provides clear leadership'. The report also stated that 'information is disseminated to all staff'. It also recognised that the Principal 'holds open forum meetings termly and issues bulletins on strategic issues'. The inspection also recognised our excellent marketing of the college locally and external relations with the local authority, employers and community groups. In brief, the recognition of the excellent work carried by staff boosted their confidence and provided us with a solid platform for further improvement.

CHAPTER ELEVEN

RETIREMENT AND RESTORATIVE JUSTICE

A significant development we embarked upon, was the expansion of our information technology provision by locating these facilities for easy access to potential users. This initiative resulted in innovative provision in Nottingham. Besides Community Centres, we developed significant IT provisions in the Queens Medical Centre (one of the largest teaching hospital in the country), Trent Bridge Cricket Ground, and in an office block opposite the Market Square in Nottingham. In addition, securing a significant European Grant, we extended our IT provision on our Clifton Campus. This was an important initiative since the College was working in collaboration with Trent University to deliver higher education courses in Multi-Media studies. In addition to the IT developments, we began to expand our service industry provision and particularly our sports provision. The college established a Basketball Academy and increasingly recruited tall students whom I had to look up to. In brief, our strategy of increasing local provision at the expense of franchising courses was on track.

Sometime after the inspection, I began to play a more active role on external educational bodies

Marching on Downing Street; members of the Association for College Management handed Tony Blair a petition this week calling for an immediate increase in staff salaries

involved with further education. The Network for Black Managers (NBM), established in 1996, was beginning to make an impact in terms of preparing Black and Asian personnel to aspire to higher roles in their respective organisations by improving their managerial skills and raising their expectations. In 1996, when I was appointed as Principal, there was only one other Black Principal in the UK and that was Wally Brown in Liverpool. Robin Landman, Rajinder Mann and Wally Brown were inspirational colleagues working in the sector and they were instrumental in establishing the NBM. I began to play a more active role in the organisation, including two stints as Chairman, and gradually we began to see more Black managers in the sector as well as a significant rise in the number of Black Principals. I was also invited to join the Department of Education's working party on Citizenship Education. In addition, I served as a trustee for a number of years on the Helena Kennedy Foundation, an influential body financially supporting aspiring students in the further education sector to achieve their vocational and educational goals. I was also involved with the Association of College Managers which included handing a petition to Number Ten, Downing Street regarding improving pay and conditions for people working in further education.

One memorable occasion in Nottingham was when I was invited to join a group of Asian politicians, including an MP, a Lord and a local councillor to talk about education and jobs prospects for young Asian people. There were nearly a thousand people attending this weekend meeting and the politicians gave their normal spiel about discrimination and difficulties for young Asian people growing up in England, When I was invited to the podium, I acknowledged the difficulties young Asian people experience regarding career prospects and discrimination but I wanted to take a different approach to the problem. I put my prepared notes away and asked the gathering a simple question – 'Please put up your hand, if in the last week, you talked to your children about their work at school and their progress ?' A very small number of hands were raised and I began my narrative about 'ascription' and their role in influencing and raising the aspirations and expectations of their respective off springs. Furthermore, I suggested that besides educational establishments, the two other groups most likely to influence aspirations of young people were young people's peer groups and parents. I went further by suggesting that if we all worked together, we could achieve much better outcomes for our young people. I was pleased that after the meeting was over, a significant number of parents came to me and thanked me for my contribution to the gathering and in particular making them more aware of their responsibilities rather than only focusing on generic race issues.

One of the most heartening occasion I witnessed at South Nottingham College serving its community, arose out of a tragic event. I was in the college one evening, after the day classes had all finished and the evening classes had not yet begun when I heard a massive explosion emanating from nearby. My immediate reaction was to go downstairs to investigate the source of this bang, thinking it could have come from one of our science laboratories. Having been assured by members of staff still then at the college that the explosion was likely to be coming from one of the houses nearby, I went outside the building to investigate further. The main site of the college during this time was located in the residential suburbs of West Bridgford, Nottingham and in close proximity of the college there was a relatively large complex of residential care bungalows for older inhabitants. We quickly gathered that the explosion emanated from one of these dwellings and that it was likely to be a gas explosion. We informed the emergency services who asked us to help evacuate the older residents from the surrounding residential properties in case there was a second explosion as a result of fractured gas pipes. We took several immediate actions – firstly, we ensured that the college car park was vacated in order for the emergency services to be accommodated; secondly, Darren who was a programme manager used the college bus to go around the estate and transfer the older residents from their homes to the college; thirdly, we accommodated all the evacuees in the college hall with staff reassuring them they were safe here and could stay as long as necessary; fourthly, the catering staff provided refreshments and ensured that the evacuees were comfortable; and fifthly we provided the emergency services with a dedicated office from which they could conduct their business without interruptions.

Shortly after, the emergency services were able to determine the cause and nature of the explosion, they informed us that it was indeed a gas explosion which resulted in one fatality. As the evening progressed, more and more members of staff came in to assist with this incident and they included a variety of support staff, office staff, teaching staff and technical staff. Many of them remained until late at night and only returned to their own homes after the emergency services informed the evacuees/ residents that it was safe to return to their homes. This tragic event demonstrated that the college was a community resource and that the members of staff fully understood the notion of 'community spirit' and were very willing to put this into action in the face of an emergency. In addition to supporting the emergency services and members of staff to assist in this emergency, I took on the role of answering calls on the switchboard. I recall that one of the calls came in from one of the television studios and they wished to know what had occurred at the college. I informed them that there was an explosion at one of the bungalows that housed older people and the college was providing support both to the residents of the estate and the emergency services. At that point, the person from the studio requested that I put her through to somebody important in the college. My reply surprised her when I stated that everyone who worked at South Nottingham College was important and could she be more specific. At this point, she asked to speak to the head of the college and my reply was one simple word 'Speaking'. This surprised her and she asked if I was not just the receptionist manning the switchboard? I explained to her that in an emergency, we all did what needed to be done and explained to her what had happened and the role a variety of people were playing to ensure that the older residents were safe and comfortable whilst the emergency services completed their work.

The following day, Darren who was on evacuation duty with the college minibus the night before told of his amusing encounter with one of the older residents. He stated that he knocked on the door of the resident and an older women, still in her dressing gown, answered and Darren informed her that she must get ready and jump into the minibus so that she would be transported safely away from the danger in the vicinity. She informed Darren that she could not do that since she had not yet watched the scheduled television episode of 'Home and Away'. Darren with his usual diplomatic skills informed her further of the potential danger she would be in if she remained in her home. Thankfully, she reluctantly abandoned her hopes of watching an episode of 'Home and Away' and arrived at the college safely, fully dressed.

Whilst my relationship with the Chair and most of the Governors was excellent, it took me almost two years to persuade the Remuneration Committee of the Governors to make a major change in the way they worked. The Remuneration Committee in Colleges, like in many other public sector bodies, determined the pay of the CEO and other senior staff of the college. In normal circumstances, these bodies usually awarded them an annual pay increase which was a few percentage points above what all/any other members of staff received. Having done some research on this, I soon came to the logical conclusion that there was no evidence that this resulted in better or worse performance by CEOs and senior staff and that there was no justification to differentiate, in percentage terms, between this cohort and the rest of the staff. I also pointed out two further factors – firstly, that senior staff and CEOs had higher salaries than the rest of the staff and any percentage increase in their salaries would result in a higher award in any case; secondly, there was no empirical evidence which suggested that if senior staff, including CEOs, were awarded the same percentage increase as the rest of the staff that they would either work with less enthusiasm or sabotage the work of the organisation. I was pleased that the Remuneration Committee and the Governors accepted my proposals of a fairer system for determining the salary of all the staff. I suspected that one or two of my senior colleagues were less enthusiastic of this development.

The other issue which concerned me, a year before I left the college, was in relation to the Governor's appointment of a new Director of Finance. Once the new director of Finance began her work at the college, it was brought to my attention by the two

P.A.s in our senior staff office that she was spending an inordinate amount of time on the phone dealing with her private business. We later learnt that she and her partner had a property portfolio and were working as private landlords in the housing market. On examining the telephone records, the P.A.s concern was justified. I raised this issue both with the Director of Finance and the Chair & Vice Chair of the Governors. The other equally disturbing issue was that she stated categorically that she was unable to do 'financial forecasts', which I considered essential for financial management. Before her probation period was over for the reasons outlined above, I suggested to the Chair and Vice Chair that we did not renew her contract. Unfortunately they assumed that there may have been other reasons, such as a personality conflict, to explain why I recommended this course of action and this was very frustrating. With hindsight, I should have then raised it with the full governing body which may have resulted in a different outcome. A footnote to this is that a little while after I departed from the college, she also left.

On the personal front, whilst my work was both demanding and satisfying, I felt a little isolated in terms of my 'free' time. By 2002 Jane and I had been living apart for five years and she had recently departed on a voluntary scheme to work in Zambia. One of the links I maintained with my previous post in Keighley was with members of staff I previously worked closely with. The communication was frequently for references, if the person was seeking a post elsewhere. My previous P.A. Liz and I occasionally communicated particularly about events in Keighley and on one occasion I invited her over to visit my college. My relationship with Liz developed from that visit and after a number of years we were married. I assumed that my remarriage may have caused some dismay and possibly anger amongst my children despite the fact that Jane and I had been living apart for many years by then. It is worth mentioning that there was no acrimony between Jane and myself and we have a fairly good relationship now. My own children and family have accepted this situation and we have a good relationship with all. On a lighter note, Liz's family including her mother paid us a lunch visit soon after we were married and I introduced myself and informed her that I came from a long line of Turkish waiters. She was a little bemused until one of the members of her family informed her that I was just pulling her leg. After lunch was over, Liz's mother informed Liz 'you must keep hold of him since he is a very good cook'. An unexpected compliment to someone who is still learning to cook today.

My developing culinary skills were severely tested on two other occasions. The College initiated a programme of hosting and teaching a cohort of Japanese students from Osaka University during the long summer vacation. The programme centred on developing multi-media skills and improving their fluency of the English language. The thirty students were accompanied by two tutors and midway through their course, I invited them over one evening for a buffet meal. The meal I prepared, assisted by my very competent 'Sous Chef', Liz, included my speciality, 'potatoes with attitude', fried rice, spicy oven baked fish, spicy chicken and a variety of vegetables – all on a very small cooker. The students and tutors enjoyed the meal and several of them commented, that whilst they enjoyed living with their respective English hosts, they really missed spicy food. Whilst they were complimentary about the food Liz and I served, they were delighted by the variety of cheesecakes we bought from a shop in West Bridgford. The students must have enjoyed their three months with us and their respective English hosts, since many of them were in tears when they departed from Nottingham on their way back to Osaka. The second occasion when my culinary skills were tested was when my brother, Ismail, his family and Kasia's cousin from Poland came to Nottingham for a meal. I was informed that one of them only ate 'halal' meat, whilst another would eat meat only if it was not halal. To complicate matters further, I was informed that there was a 'vegan' in the group as well. Since I had neither the experience or knowledge of cooking for vegans before, I was on a very steep learning curve and scoured the local shops for suitable vegan foods. Somehow, I managed this unusual challenge and by the smiles on the photograph below, I may have been marginally successful.

Back to 2002 when I made several decisions to prepare for retirement – firstly, I asked our Human Resources department to obtain from the Teachers' Pension Fund what I would expect on retirement in the summer of 2002 and this was very satisfactory; and secondly, I purchased a holiday home in Northern Cyprus to enjoy my retirement. About this time, one of the more distressing stressful elements of working as a Principal occurred when thieves

From (r to l) Krystina from Poland, Neil, Kasia, Ismail, Sara, Adam and me.

broke into our Clifton Campus, an isolated campus away from residential areas several times and on the last occasion, by driving their van into the glass fronted computer and multi media room. They stole over £100,000 worth of equipment and created significant damage and disruption to the work of students and staff. The stolen equipment could not be replaced immediately and I was at my wits' end to work out a solution in order that the students were not disadvantaged in their final year assessment. Working urgently with all relevant agencies, we were able to replace most of the equipment as well as employ security officers for night and weekend duty on the campus.

During the early years after the Learning and

Skills Council (LSC) replaced the Further Education Funding Council, it extolled the virtues of working through 'partnership and trust' with colleges and other providers. Whilst I had some reservations with this creatively ambiguous concept, as a Principal of a very successful College I could, I felt, cope with this ambiguity and subscribe to the underlying principles of working in partnership in an environment of mutual trust and respect. My experience as Principal between December 2002 and January 2003 undermined not only these fundamental tenets of sound management but also my belief in 'fair play and justice' through the behaviour and conduct of the Executive Director of the Nottinghamshire Learning and Skills Council, Rob Valentine, directed at me personally. There may have been several reasons for his hostility towards me – I raised issues of concern at regional LSC meetings when others remained silent. My decision to opt out of talks of merger may also have contributed to his animosity. I raised this at this point because what transpired subsequently was, I believe, a direct result of this underlying antagonism directed at me personally. A specific example of this is when there was a meeting between the LSC, three Governors and myself to discuss LSC support, I raised the issue that I was experiencing some difficulties with a new senior member of our finance team without inviting comment. I was then shocked by the unwarranted malicious remark by Rob Valentine 'If I was in your position I would chuck myself in the river'.

I was asked by the College's Governing body to arrange a meeting with the Nottinghamshire LSC to explore the possibility of short term financial support, in the event it was needed, to avoid a potential cash flow problem becoming a reality and to preserve our capital reserves – in brief, to phase the money we needed to return to the LSC over 6 months at most. At a brief preliminary meeting, I was asked to prepare three papers for discussion on 20 December 2002. The three papers were prepared and sent to the LSC and on 19 December 2002, I received an email from the Finance Director stating 'Ahmed, Thank you for the information that you supplied to Rob last night. It was very helpful!' The papers clearly indicated that even after returning the money to the LSC for not meeting the targets set by them, we still had a positive, albeit, a small cash reserve. Our cash flow forecast also clearly indicated that even after returning all the money to the LSC, our cash reserves would be restored to a healthy £1m within 6 months. The papers also indicated the measures the college would take to achieve all this without compromising the quality of provision.

A few minutes before the meeting between the three College Governors, myself and the LSC commenced, my two P.A.s noted the aggressive tone Rob Valentine had adopted whilst in the waiting area. As soon as the formal meeting commenced, the hostility and belligerence was evident and the LSC officers, headed by Rob Valentine refused to discuss the papers prepared for the meeting without giving any reason. This behaviour was in clear breach of procedures outlined in the National LSC Circular 02/06. My track record in terms of managing College finance and the College's academic achievements were ignored – on becoming Principal, for instance, I turned a large deficit into a healthy surplus in a relatively short space of time; that when we secured a large 10 year bank loan for a rebuilding programme, we repaid this in 18 months; reduced our dependency on franchising work from 48% to 8% . In terms of teaching and learning and the quality of our further and higher education provision we were recognised as excellent by inspectors and assessors. Our rigorous customer survey indicated year-on-year improvements. I also discovered subsequently that whilst my College did not have a deficit at all, a neighbouring large college in Nottingham was several million pounds in the red and that no major action took place regarding this college or its principal, senior management or governors of this college. In addition, I was also informed that six months after my departure, the college implemented a reorganisation plan not very different to the one I submitted to the local LSC in December 2002.

At the end of this very brief meeting, I informed the Governors present, including the Chair, of my intention to resign on the basis that I could no longer work with the local LSC under Rob Valentine particularly when I was personally subjected to unwarranted and unreasonable hostility. As events unfolded, I suspected that there was a 'fifth columnist' connected to the College working in cahoots with local LSC officers to undermine my position. After spending my first short holiday in my new retirement home in Cyprus, I submitted my resignation as Principal in January 2003. I was pleasantly surprised to receive a significant number of supportive emails, letters, cards and telephone calls from sector Principals and other colleagues.

I was surprised and touched when significant numbers of staff told me that they were saddened by my resignation. Meeting officers of community organisations expressing similar sentiments was very reassuring that the college worked productively with its community. I was pleasantly surprised when the trade union representatives in the College came to see me to express their regrets that I was leaving since they stated that our relationship was always based on respect and trust and that I always negotiated with them in an open and honest manner.

As a result of my experience, I made a formal complaint to the then Chief Executive of the national LSC. My complaint centred on two specific issues: firstly the conduct and behaviour of Rob Valentine towards me personally and secondly, that the local LSC intervention in subsequent college affairs was tantamount to 'Ultra Vires' (outside its legal authority) and in clear breach of procedures stated in their own Circular 02/06.

After leaving the college I was offered lucrative consultancy work but after a short period of time, I decided this was not what I wanted to do. I was also invited to consider, by a consultancy firm, a Principal's post in a very large College of Further and Higher Education in the North West, with a salary almost twice of what I was paid at my previous college, on a two year contract whilst the college went through a major reorganisation. I felt pleased with the offers but decided that I no longer wished to work full time in any capacity and began gradually to adjust to my new life.

A neighbouring local LSC Executive Director

was appointed to carry out an investigation into my complaint. I rejected his brief report since it did not satisfactorily address either of the two issues I highlighted in my complaint. Around this time, the Chief Executive of the national LSC changed and I stated clearly to the LSC's legal representative that if they did not take my complaint seriously, I would have no other option but to seek a judicial review. In addition to this, I also wrote a centre piece in the NBM Newsletter, which had widespread coverage in the sector, explaining the reasons why I resigned from my post. My further representation to the LSC resulted in an independent investigator being appointed. I was asked what was the outcome I desired from his investigation? I think he was expecting me to state something regarding financial compensation, but I was very clear of the outcome I wanted: I wanted the Executive Director of the Nottinghamshire LSC dismissed. On a sector wide basis, the introduction of clear guidelines of the roles of executive directors and the establishment of an independent, transparent and accountable investigation system for complaints, in which the whole sector has confidence.

In January 2004, on the day the report of my complaint was to be published, I was delighted to be informed that the new Chief Executive of the national Learning and Skills Council had acted decisively and dismissed Rob Valentine, the Executive Director of the Nottinghamshire Learning and Skills Council and his deputy, the Director of Finance. I felt that my quiet, controlled and logical approach to this emotionally draining episode resulted in a very satisfactory conclusion. I felt vindicated by this sudden turn of events and it provided me with the confidence to continue working in the sector on a voluntary basis, particularly as Chair of the very successful Network for Black Managers and its major work, The Black Leadership Initiative. The Network, The Association of Colleges and the Times Educational Supplement were all very supportive in regards to my complaint. I was pleasantly surprised and pleased that during the next Association of Colleges Conference, several serving Principals of Colleges came up to me to state that they were pleased with the outcome of my complaint and that this gave them more confidence working in the sector. Besides thanking them, I stated I was pleased that my persistence paid off and now I could finally banish this large demon from my professional life.

CHAPTER TWELVE

AND THEN

One year after my retirement and with a more than satisfactory outcome from my complaint, I felt I could now enjoy working in the sector on a voluntary basis as well as enjoy the company of family and friends without the constraints of work. Besides supporting the work of the Network of Black Managers and witnessing the growth in numbers of senior managers and Principals from BAME communities, I began to look forward to spending more time with family (both in the UK and South Africa) and exploring the beauty of Northern Cyprus and its history. During this period, Liz and I made two trips to South Africa and besides visiting friends and family, it gave me the opportunity to show Liz the environment I grew up in as well as enjoy the country and its outstanding landscape. Liz made a lasting impression on my family and now, every time I make a phone call to South Africa, my family are more interested in Liz's health and welfare than mine. In addition to these two visits to South Africa, I was also a member of a small delegation to promote greater collaboration between South African and English Colleges.

The year 2004 is a memorable year for the family since it was in August of that year that all the brothers and sister gathered in one place for the first time in our lives. My late brother 'Doc' made a significant effort by encouraging my brothers in South Africa and brother in Canada to come to Manchester for a unique family reunion. As I intimated earlier, during my childhood, one or more of my brothers was/were studying abroad and therefore we were never together in one place at one time. The reunion in Manchester allowed us the opportunity to meet in person and share some of our stories growing up either in South Africa or abroad. The photograph below was taken on the day of our reunion but unfortunately my sister Bibi and brother Gulam are not present for some inexplicable reason in the photograph but were present on the day.

By now, Liz and I were enjoying our regular breaks

From left to right: 'Doc', Joe, Mahmood, Me, Ebrahim, and Ismail

Picture of the Six Brothers Wives, Children and Grandchildren (Most of the Clan)

to Cyprus and discovering the unspoilt natural beauty of this divided country. We also began the process of building up a network of friends of a similar age and circumstances locally. I should state at this point that the bungalow we purchased was one of five on the site with a large shared swimming pool. Three of the other owners were also from abroad – two from the U.K. and one from Canada. The fifth bungalow was owned by the Developer who eventually sold it to another U.K. resident. After a couple of years the floor of the large shared swimming pool disintegrated with a large crack and the Developer, who had by now moved out, refused to take responsibility for the poor workmanship and damage. The owners of bungalow number 3, Lorna from Dundee, bungalow 2, Mel and Laurrayne from Blackburn, and Liz and I decided to sue the Developer for the full cost of replacing the large swimming pool. Whilst we were still enjoying holidaying in Cyprus, the attendance in court at irregular intervals was time consuming and slow. After over two years and multiple attendances in court preparing and giving evidence, the judges found in our favour and awarded us the full cost of replacing the pool. Having spearheaded the action, I was delighted by the outcome. I thought that retirement would have excluded recourse to complaints and waiting for decisions and outcomes, but alas the unpredictable has never had a timescale.

In addition to enjoying our visits to Cyprus and elsewhere, I now had the opportunity to get pleasure from the company of grandchildren through marriage. Harry, Jake and Tom were the first grandchildren to spend some of their summer holidays with us in Nottingham. Their visit gave us the opportunity to explore the area more extensively and on one of our outings an unfortunate accident occurred. We were driving back home with all three of the boys in the rear seats of the car, all with their seat belts fastened, and I was stationary awaiting a Land Rover with an attached trailer, slowly turning left when a car rammed into us from the rear. Obviously, besides the shock, my first concern was the well being of all the passengers and the driver of the recalcitrant car. Fortunately all the passengers in both cars, whilst shaken, were fine and the driver of the offending vehicle accepted full responsibility for the accident. The most memorable part of the accident was when the boys said 'This is the first time we have been in an accident and this is important since it will give us an opportunity, when we return to school, to write something different about our holidays compared to all our classmates'. We now also regularly enjoy the company of George and Leila and they continue to amuse us with their quick wit and sense of humour. Evie and Fletcher, the other two grandchildren have visited us occasionally and impressed us with their acrobatics and energy.

During the next few years, besides being actively involved with the NBM, I also took the opportunity to write on topical educational issues occasionally in either the Times Educational Supplement or the NBM Newsletter. In 2005, in the wake of the London bombing, I wrote about the danger of 'islamaphobia'. Later, for instance, I wrote an article for the TES entitled 'Let's focus on our common ground.' which is as pertinent today as it was then. I stated that with a family made up of a variety of different faiths, we go beyond mere tolerance: we have mutual respect for the deeply held beliefs of others... We consider and value their contributions and the factors that bind us together in common humanity, rather than accentuate those elements that differentiate us. Other TES published articles included 'Harness the power of positive role models' and one more provocative article focussing on College Remuneration Committees entitled 'Are paymasters just feeding unfairness?' This is pertinent today and applicable to many different public bodies and not only to colleges.

David Collins, my University friend and his wife Doctor Erica Collins, kept in touch and they usually stopped with us in Nottingham on their way to the North East. In 2008, Erica informed me that David was very ill and Liz and I visited him in Portsmouth. The visit was a difficult one for me since the David I was familiar with, a vibrant and energetic person, was a shadow of his former self. The thing I still recollect vividly from that visit was when his whole face lit up when I mentioned the warm and wonderful rapport between his sons, Richard and Andy, their respective wives and their mother Erica. A month later, David passed away. I mention this here since David was not only a great friend of mine but he was an important influence on my beliefs and values.

With regard to my own children, I am very pleased and proud with their progress in their respective lives. Amy, despite the difficulties she encountered in her earlier life, has been living an independent life, with the significant support of Jane, her friends locally and to smaller extent from Liz and me, for over fifteen years. Esme and Joseph are politically active and prolific writers. Esme has co-authored a book, works as a paramedic and provides considerable support to her delightful partner, Yuri, who has had a lung transplant. In addition to all this, she is also studying for a higher degree. Joseph also has a very active political life and is an author of two books. Besides speaking at a variety of meetings, both at home and abroad, he is just completing his doctorate. My only concern about them is that I do not see them as regularly as I was hoping to.

In the summer of 2012, before embarking on our planned visit to Canada, I was pleased that Liz and I visited my brother 'Doc' in Manchester since he was ill. Our visit to Canada in July 2012 commenced in Toronto and this gave me the opportunity to renew my friendship with 'Cas' Bhabha from South Africa – the last time we met was when he stayed with me in Manchester in 1962. We travelled from Toronto to

Montreal and spent some delightful times with my brother Mahmood and his children and their families. We then departed for Quebec where we joined up with our Cyprus/Canada friends, Bob and Jenny, for a few days. Whilst in Quebec, I received a deeply distressing email that my brother 'Doc' passed away and besides making frantic phone calls to England, I sat in my hotel room quietly and remembered the kindness he bestowed upon me when I was living with the family in Manchester. After Quebec, Jenny and Bob drove us to Nova Scotia to their home to enjoy the beauty and openness of this vast province. They were very generous hosts and our visit to Nova Scotia was a memorable one.

Shortly after these events, I was pleased to receive a letter from the Cabinet Office inviting me to Investiture at Buckingham Palace to be awarded an OBE for Services to Further Education. In addition to Liz, I was delighted that my brother Ismail, who was instrumental in my coming to the UK to further my own education, and my nephew, Khursheed representing my late brother, 'Doc' were able to join me for this celebratory occasion.

Whilst I was pleased to be awarded an OBE for services to further education, I have to acknowledge the enormous contribution my family and all the colleagues I worked with over 34 years in further and higher education had made, to make this possible. Shortly after receiving the award, Liz and I departed to Cyprus for our normal winter break. We had no idea that any of our friends in Northern Cyprus were aware that I received an OBE. When we approached our home, all the lights were off and it was pitch

With Liz outside The Palace

dark. As soon as we turned into the driveway, all the lights, including some very colourful lights came on and we were stunned by a large banner hung, by the entrance, with 'Congratulations OBE' in large letters scrolled on it. This was then followed by a surprise party. This was a wonderful surprise arranged by our generous and kind hearted friends and this was the real highlight to be awarded an OBE.

After returning from Cyprus, Liz and I were invited by Nottinghamshire County Council to celebrate with other County award winners. It was a real pleasure to meet so many award winners from the field of sports and the community, all of whom made a significant contribution in their own way and were recognised nationally and locally for that. The award also gave me the opportunity to participate on several occasions on the BBC Radio programme locally not only on receiving an OBE but also on my views when Nelson Mandela passed away, and the contribution he made

to my country of birth. This was an 'add on' I did not anticipate but it provided me with an opportunity to reflect on my early life in South Africa and how fortunate I was to be given a chance to rebuild my life in England. My encounter with events, including my head trauma in South Africa, and subsequent life in England have, without a doubt, influenced my life and provided me with an unshakable faith and belief in the kindness and generosity of people including family members, friends, colleagues, neighbours and perfect strangers. In this unsettled world, I value this and I am thankful that this occurs more frequently than is reported.